CHECK YOUR VOCABULARY ENGLISH WORKBOOK FOR STUDENTS

a workbook for users

by Rawdon Wyatt

انتشارات زبانکده

نماینده انحصاری انتشارات LONGMAN در ایران

مرکز فروش و پخش انواع کتب و نوارهای Higher Education, E.L.T

و جدیدترین متد سمعی و بصری آموزش زبان

تهران ـ میدان انقلاب ـ بازارچه کتاب ـ شماره ۸   تلفن: ۶۴۰۲۳۶۷   فکس: ۶۴۹۲۹۶۱

e-mail zabankadeh @ sinasoft.net   صندوق پستی ۵۶۴ ـ ۱۳۱۴۵

PETER COLLIN PUBLISHING

First published in Great Britain 1999
by Peter Collin Publishing Ltd
1 Cambridge Road, Teddington, Middlesex, UK

© Peter Collin Publishing Ltd 1999

British Library Cataloguing in Publication Data
A Catalogue record for this book is available from the British Library
ISBN 1-901659-11-9

Text computer typeset by PCP Ltd
Printed by Blackmore, UK

COMPANION TITLES TO THIS WORKBOOK

English Dictionary for Students	1-901659-06-2
English Thesaurus for Students	1-901659-31-3
English Workbook for Students	1-901659-11-9

TITLES IN THE SERIES

Check your:

Vocabulary for Banking & Finance	0-948549-96-3
Vocabulary for Business, 2nd ed	1-901659-27-5
Vocabulary for Computing, 2nd ed	1-901659-28-3
Vocabulary for Colloquial English	0-948549-97-1
Vocabulary for Hotels, Tourism, Catering	0-948549-75-0
Vocabulary for Law, 2nd ed	1-901659-21-6
Vocabulary for Medicine	0-948549-59-9

English Dictionaries:

Dictionary of Accounting	0-948549-27-0
Dictionary of Aeronautical English	1-901659-10-0
Dictionary of Agriculture, 2nd ed	0-948549-78-5
Dictionary of American Business	0-948549-11-4
Dictionary of Automobile Engineering	0-948549-66-1
Dictionary of Banking & Finance, 2nd ed	1-901659-30-5
Dictionary of Business, 2nd ed	0-948549-51-3
Dictionary of Computing, 3rd ed	1-901659-04-6
Dictionary of Ecology & Environment, 3rd	0-948549-74-2
Dictionary of Government & Politics 2nd ed	0-948549-89-0
Dictionary of Hotels, Tourism, Catering	0-948549-40-8
Dictionary of Human Resources, 2nd ed	0-948549-79-3
Dictionary of Information Technology, 2nd	0-948549-88-2
Dictionary of Law, 2nd ed	0-948549-33-5
Dictionary of Library & Information	0-948549-68-8
Dictionary of Marketing, 2nd ed	0-948549-73-4
Dictionary of Medicine, 2nd ed	0-948549-36-X
Dictionary of Military Terms	1-901659-24-0
Dictionary of Printing & Publishing	0-948549-09-2
Dictionary of Science & Technology	0-948549-67-X

For sample pages and further information, visit our web site: **www.pcp.co.uk**
To order any of our titles, contact your local book shop or order direct from:
Peter Collin Publishing Ltd
1 Cambridge Road, Teddington, Middx, TW11 8DT, UK
tel: 0208 943 3386 fax: 0208 943 1673 email: info@pcp.co.uk

Contents

About this workbook

This workbook is designed to help you in two ways.

1. It helps you to use your *English Dictionary for Students (ISBN 1-901659-06-2, published by Peter Collin Publishing)* more efficiently: you will learn to recognise how words are presented, what they mean, how to find other forms of the same word, how they are pronounced and how to locate other information which you will find useful or interesting.

2. It helps you to develop your knowledge of word forms, individual words, phrasal verbs and idiomatic and colloquial expressions so that you will be able to communicate more effectively in English.

The workbook is divided into seven sections.

Section 1.
Finding your way around the dictionary. This shows the different features of the dictionary and what they mean. You should do the tasks in this section before you do anything else in this workbook.

Section 2.
Word forms. This shows you how to change common words so that they have a different meaning or a different grammatical function.

Section 3.
Topics. Theme-based units help you to develop your vocabulary for different areas, eg, money, shopping, etc.

Section 4.
Phrasal verbs. The most important phrasal verbs are presented and practised in alphabetical order according to their main verb.

Section 5.
Pronunciation. This section will help you to become familiar with the phonetic symbols used to show how a word is pronounced.

Section 6.
Record sheets. These are photocopiable sheets on which you can record word forms, vocabulary items and phrasal verbs. You should keep these in your files for future reference, or for when you need to revise language points for an exam.

Section 7.
Answers. You should usually be able to find the answers to all the tasks in your dictionary. You should not look at the answers until you have tried to do each task using just your dictionary to help you.

From time to time, you will see these symbols:
📖 (followed by a page number). This means that you will find more information on the same topic on another page in the workbook.

☞ (followed by a word). This shows you where to look in your dictionary to find the meaning of an unusual or difficult word.

Glossary

The following words and expressions are used in this book and/or in the dictionary. Refer to these pages if you come across these words and are not sure what they mean.

- **abstract noun**
  An abstract noun is a noun that we cannot usually see, hear, touch, smell or taste. Examples include *arrangement*, *choice* and *possibility*. **There is a <u>possibility</u> that the <u>arrangement</u> we make won't be that of your first <u>choice</u>.** The opposite of an abstract noun is a *concrete noun*.

- **adjective**
  An adjective is a word which describes a noun. Examples include *big*, *black* and *hairy*. **I stared in horror at the <u>big</u>, <u>black</u>, <u>hairy</u> spider walking across the floor.**

- **adverb**
  A adverb is a word which modifies a verb, an adjective, another adverb or a whole sentence. Examples include *slowly*, *very* and *badly*. **He walked <u>slowly</u> because the snow was <u>very</u> thick and he had already fallen <u>badly</u> a couple of times.**

- **apostrophe**
  An apostrophe is the punctuation mark '. It either shows that a letter has been left out of a word (eg, weren't) or is used with *s* to show possession (eg, Brian's book). With singular words, the apostrophe comes before the *s* (eg, a boy's coat). With plural words the apostrophe comes after the *s* (eg, the girls' team).

- **auxiliary verb**
  An auxiliary verb is a verb which forms part of a verb phrase. There are three auxiliary verbs in English: *be*, *do* and *have*. **I <u>have</u> just seen John. He <u>was</u> eating lunch. <u>Did</u> you tell him he was supposed to be at school?**

- **colloquialism**
  A colloquialism is an expression which is used in common speech (usually informal) where the words do not have their literal meaning. For example, *to kick the bucket* means *to die*.

- **comparative**
  This is the form of an adjective or adverb which shows comparison between two things. Comparatives are either formed by adding -*er* to a word (eg, her car is cheap*er* than mine) or by preceding the word with *more* (eg, my car is *more* expensive than her's).

- **compound adjective**
  A compound adjective is an adjective made up of more than one word. For example, a *five-star* hotel.

- **compound noun**
  A compound noun is a noun made up of more than one word. For example, a *birthday party*.

- **conjunction**
  A conjunction is a word which links different sections of a sentence. Examples include *and* and *although*.
  <u>Although</u> he left early, he was late <u>and</u> missed his train.

- **countable noun**
  A countable noun is a noun which can have both singular and plural forms (eg, dog / dogs, game / games, man / men.

- **idiom**
  An idiom is an expression where the words do not have their literal meaning. For example, it's raining *cats and dogs* means that it's raining *heavily*.

- **irregular verb**
  An irregular verb is a verb that does not usually end with -*ed* in its past simple or past participle forms. *Eat*, *run* and *sing* are examples of irregular verbs.

- **modal verb**
  A modal verb is a verb used with another verb to show permission, intention, duty etc. They are sometimes called *modal auxiliaries* or just *modals*. *Can*, *can't* and *should* are modal verbs.

© Peter Collin Publishing Ltd, 1999
Based on the *English Dictionary for Students*, ISBN 1-901659-06-2

You <u>can</u> use the library, but you <u>can't</u> take books out and you <u>should</u> tell the librarian if you damage a book.

For a complete list of modal verbs, see the entry for '*modal*' in your dictionary.

- **object**
  An object is a noun or pronoun which follows directly from a verb or preposition. **The cat caught the mouse.** *Mouse* is the object of the verb *caught*.

- **phonemes**
  A phoneme is a single speech sound that makes a word different from another word. For example, the words *bed* and *red* differ only in their initial sound: *bed* begins with a /b/ and *red* begins with a /r/. Therefore, /b/ and /r/ are English phonemes.
  Phonemes are represented as symbols after each key entry in the dictionary. It is important that you familiarise yourself with them because many letters in English can be pronounced in more than one way.

- **phrasal verb**
  A phrasal verb is a combination of a verb with a preposition. This combination often changes the main meaning of the verb (eg, John *takes after* his brother. *Takes after* means *looks like*)

- **plural**
  More than one. For example, *boats* is the plural of *boat*. Not all plurals end with -s. For example, *children* is the plural of *child*. Your dictionary will tell you if this is the case.

- **prefix**
  A prefix is part of a word put in front of another to form a new word. *Anti-* , *re-* and *dis-* are examples of prefixes. **The football team was <u>dis</u>qualified for <u>anti</u>social behaviour, but later <u>re</u>-admitted to the competition.**

- **pronoun**
  A pronoun is a word used instead of a noun. *I, she, it* and *they* are examples of <u>subject</u> pronouns. *Me, her* and *them* are examples of <u>object</u> pronouns.

- **proverb**
  A proverb is a saying which teaches you something. For example, *the early bird catches the worm* is a proverb which means that if you decide quickly, you will succeed.

- **regular verb**
  A regular verb is a verb which ends with *-ed* in its past simple or past participle form. *Walk, play* and *laugh* are examples of regular verbs.

- **singular noun**
  Only one. For example, *a dog, a computer*.

- **slang**
  Slang is a popular word or phrase used by certain groups of people. For example, *a banger* is a slang word for either *an old car* or *a sausage*.

- **subject**
  A subject is a noun or pronoun which usually comes before a verb and shows the person or thing that does the action expressed by the verb. **The cat sat on the mat.** *The cat* is the subject of the verb *sat*.

- **suffix**
  Part of a word added to the end of a word to make another word. *-ful, -ing,* and *-ous* are examples of suffixes. **Be care<u>ful</u> not to call his lessons bor<u>ing</u>; he can be danger<u>ous</u> when angry.**

- **superlative**
  This is the form of an adjective or adverb which shows the most or the least when talking about quantity, quality or intensity. Superlatives are formed either by adding *-est* to a word (eg, what's the fast*est* animal in the world?) or by preceding the word with *most* (eg, It's one of the *most* expensive cars on the market).

- **uncountable noun**
  An uncountable noun is a noun which cannot have a plural form (eg, homework, rice, cream).

- **verb**
  A verb is a word which shows an action, being or feeling etc. **She <u>felt</u> angry, so she <u>hit</u> him with her fist.**

© Peter Collin Publishing Ltd, 1999
Based on the *English Dictionary for Students*, ISBN 1-901659-06-2

Getting started: Your needs

1. YOUR NEEDS.

Do this task with a partner. Look at the list of reasons for using a dictionary and put them in order of importance (1 = the most important, 13 = the least important). Tell your partner why you chose this order.

Order of Importance

A.	To check the spelling of words.
B.	To find out how to pronounce words.
C.	To learn new words.
D.	To find out the meanings of words that you see in, for example, a book or magazine.
E.	To find out whether a word has more than one meaning.
F.	To find out how one word works with another.
G.	To find out the different forms of a word (eg, adverb, adjective, etc).
H.	To find out the meanings of phrasal verbs.
I.	To learn new phrasal verbs.
J.	To find out the meanings of idioms and colloquialisms.
K.	To find out the grammatical function of a word (eg, if it is a noun or an adjective) or to find out if there are any grammatical rules connected with that word (eg, if it is followed by a plural verb).
L.	To learn new idioms and colloquialisms.
M.	To identify the difference between British-English words and American- English words.

📖*Now look at the guide on the next page.*

2. QUIZ

Do this quiz with a partner. For each question, decide TRUE or FALSE.

1. The best way to learn new vocabulary is to read the dictionary and try to remember as many words as possible.

2. A dictionary will help you to find out how to pronounce a word.

3. You should use a dictionary to find out the meanings of <u>all</u> new words that you see in, eg, a book or magazine.

4. You should always keep a written record of new words, and try to use these words whenever possible.

5. It is not enough to recognize the meaning of a word; you should be able to use it as well in your written and spoken English.

6. Knowing the meaning of a word is not enough; you must also know how it is used (ie, what words it is used with, in what situation, etc.).

7. If you are doing the Cambridge First Certificate or C.A.E. exam you are allowed to use a dictionary in the exam.

📖 *Now look at the answer key on the next page.*

© Peter Collin Publishing Ltd, 1999
Based on the *English Dictionary for Students*, ISBN 1-901659-06-2

Getting started: Guide

1. YOUR NEEDS.

Everybody has a different reason for using a dictionary, and your needs are probably different from those of your partner. While you are studying English, you will probably need to look at all of the areas covered on the previous page at some time or other.

A. Spelling mistakes are easy to make. Poor spelling can make your written English difficult to understand and if you are doing an exam, might lose you marks, especially if you make a lot of mistakes. Always use the dictionary to check your spelling, especially with longer words.

B. Unlike many other languages, one letter in English can be pronounced in many different ways. The dictionary shows how each word is pronounced. (📖 *Pages 6 + 83 - 90*)

C. This workbook, used together with the dictionary, will help you to learn new words and expressions. (📖 *Pages 22 - 73*)

D. For many students, this is the most important reason for using a dictionary.

E. A lot of English words have more than one meaning. This dictionary shows you the most commonly-used meaning, followed by the other meanings in descending order.(📖 *Page 7*)

F. This dictionary gives examples of words and expressions in sentences so that you can see how the words work with other words.

G. This dictionary shows the different forms (derivatives) of a word and gives examples of most forms in a sentence. (📖 *Pages 8, 10 - 11 + 13 - 21*)

H. This dictionary shows the ways in which a verb can be combined with a preposition or prepositions to make a phrasal verb (📖 *Pages 8 + 75 - 82*).

I. The book will help you to develop a 'bank' of the most important phrasal verbs (📖 *Page 94*).

J. An idiom is a phrase which is often difficult to understand from the meanings of the separate words. Colloquialisms are expressions that we usually only use in spoken English. In the dictionary, idioms and colloquialisms are explained separately in the entry.

K. The dictionary tells you the grammatical function of each word (📖 *Pages 6 - 7*) and if there are any other special grammatical rules connected with a word.

L. The workbook will help you to develop a 'bank' of the most important words, including idioms, colloquialisms and other expressions (📖 *Page 93*)

M. The dictionary tells you if a word or expression is British or American. (📖 *Pages 12 + 26-27*).

2. QUIZ

1. FALSE. The best way to learn new vocabulary is to read books, magazines and newspapers and use the dictionary to check the meanings of any words or expressions that you don't know.

2. TRUE. But you must know how to read the pronunciation symbols (we call these *phonetic symbols*) that you find after each entry. (📖 *Pages 6 + 83 - 90*).

3. FALSE. It is not always necessary to look up the meaning of a word. Very often, you should be able to guess the meaning of a new word by looking at the words around it (we call this the *context*).

4. TRUE. Try to develop a 'bank' of new words and expressions and 'recycle' them in your spoken and written English. Otherwise, you will forget most of them very quickly. (📖 *Pages 92 - 94*)

5. TRUE. The more vocabulary you have at your command, the easier and more effectively you will be able to communicate with other English speakers, whether you are writing or speaking.

6. TRUE. Words 'work' with one another to create meaning, and if you use the wrong words, it can be difficult for other people to understand what you mean. Your dictionary gives examples of most words in a sentence so that you can see how they work with other words.

7. FALSE. You cannot use a dictionary in these exams, which is why it is important for you to develop, recycle and remember vocabulary as much as possible.

© Peter Collin Publishing Ltd, 1999
Based on the *English Dictionary for Students*, ISBN 1-901659-06-2

Finding your way around the dictionary

The next four pages are designed to help you become familiar with the layout and main points of your PCP *English Dictionary for Students*. If you do the tasks that accompany some of the sections, you will be able to use the dictionary more efficiently. Some of the sections are cross-referenced to units later on in this workbook that will help you to develop and enlarge your English vocabulary - these are shown with a 📖 symbol and a page number / numbers.

1. THE MAIN WORD.

The main word, or *headword*, is the word that you are looking up in the dictionary. Main words are in alphabetical order in the dictionary. The main word in this case is **look.**

> **look** [lʊk] **1** *noun* **(a)** seeing something with your eyes; *have a good look at this photograph and tell me if you recognise anyone in it*; *we only had time for a quick look round the town* **(b)** the way someone or something appears; *there is a French look about her clothes*; **good looks** = pleasing and beautiful appearance; *his good looks and charm attracted many women*

2. PHONETIC SYMBOLS

Phonetic symbols are symbols which show you how each word is pronounced. (📖 *Pronunciation, pages 83 - 90*)

> **look** [lʊk] **1** *noun* **(a)** seeing something with your eyes; *have a good look at this photograph and tell me if you recognise anyone in it*; *we only had time for a quick look round the town* **(b)** the way someone or something appears; *there is a French look about her clothes*; **good looks** = pleasing and beautiful appearance; *his good looks and charm attracted many women*

3. GRAMMATICAL FUNCTION

Each main word is followed by the grammatical function of that word. If a word has more than one grammatical function. then each one is numbered. **Look** has two functions; it can either be a noun or a verb.

> **look** [lʊk] **1** *noun* **(a)** seeing something with your eyes; *have a good look at this photograph and tell me if you recognise anyone in it*; *we only had time for a quick look round the town* **(b)** the way someone or something appears; *there is a French look about her clothes*; **good looks** = pleasing and beautiful appearance; *his good looks and charm attracted many women* **(c)** searching for something; *we had a good look for the ring and couldn't find it anywhere* **2** *verb* **(a)** to turn your eyes towards something; *I want you to look carefully at this photograph*; *look in the restaurant and see if there are any tables free*; *if you look out of the office window you can see our house*

PRACTICE (A)
How many grammatical functions do the following words have?

deliberate	degenerate	stock	straight	behind

PRACTICE (B)
Match the words on the left with their grammatical function on the right.

and	article
happy	verb
sadly	preposition
come	adverb
London	pronoun
into	conjunction
me	object pronoun
the	proper noun
mine	adjective

PRACTICE (C)
Look at the following sentences. Each sentence has a word in **bold**, and a corresponding word or words with that grammatical function somewhere else in the same sentence. Identify the word(s) in each case.

Example:
It's easy to find the **article** in this sentence.
Answer = *the*

Now try these:

1. Look for the **verb** in this sentence.
2. Can you see a **preposition** hidden somewhere in this sentence?
3. You should find the **adverb** easily in this sentence.
4. I think this is a sentence that has got three **pronouns**.
5. A **conjunction** is a small but important word.
6. I bet you £10 you won't find the **object pronoun** here.
7. **Adjectives** are useful words.

4. DEFINITION
A definition is the meaning of a word; it shows the meaning of the main word and gives an example of the word in a sentence. If a word has more than one definition, then each one is given a letter.

look [luk] **1** *noun* **(a)** seeing something with your eyes; *have a good look at this photograph and tell me if you recognise anyone in it; we only had time for a quick look round the town* **(b)** the way someone or something appears; *there is a French look about her clothes;* **good looks** = pleasing and beautiful appearance; *his good looks and charm attracted many women* **(c)** searching for something; *we had a good look for the ring and couldn't find it anywhere* **2** *verb* **(a)** to turn your eyes towards something; *I want you to look carefully at this photograph; look in the restaurant and see if there are any tables free; if you look out of the office window you can see our house; he opened the lid the box and looked inside* **(b)** **to look someone in the eye** = to look straight at someone in a confident way; *he didn't dare look me in the eye*

PRACTICE.
How many definitions do the following words have?

look	invent	iron	triangle	make	do

5. DERIVATIVES

Some words can change their grammatical function (eg, from a noun to an adjective or adverb) by the addition or removal of letters, either at the end or the beginning of the word. These words are called *derivatives*. Derivatives in which the <u>end</u> of the word changes can usually be found <u>before</u> or <u>after</u> the main entry. Derivatives in which letters are added to the <u>beginning</u> of the word will usually be found in the entry for the added letters (the most important ones are *dis-* , *il-* , *im-* , *in-* and *un-* : 📖 *Word forms, pages 13 - 21*)

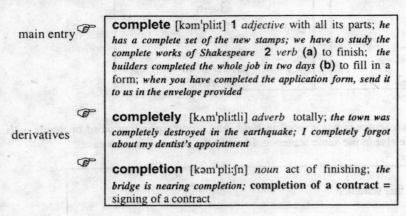

main entry ☞

complete [kəm'pliːt] **1** *adjective* with all its parts; *he has a complete set of the new stamps; we have to study the complete works of Shakespeare* **2** *verb* **(a)** to finish; *the builders completed the whole job in two days* **(b)** to fill in a form; *when you have completed the application form, send it to us in the envelope provided*

derivatives ☞

completely [kʌm'pliːtli] *adverb* totally; *the town was completely destroyed in the earthquake; I completely forgot about my dentist's appointment*

☞ **completion** [kəm'pliːʃn] *noun* act of finishing; *the bridge is nearing completion;* **completion of a contract =** signing of a contract

PRACTICE
How many derivatives can you find for the following words?

act	agree	bore	continue	satisfy	hope	decide

6. PHRASAL VERBS

A phrasal verb is the main word (ie, a verb) plus one or two prepositions. The addition of the preposition often changes the meaning of the verb. Some phrasal verbs can have more than one definition. Phrasal verbs are sometimes called *multi-word verbs*.
(📖 *Phrasal verbs, pages 75 - 82*)

Phrasal verb ☞

look back ['lʊk 'bæk] *verb* **(a)** to turn your head to see what is behind you; *he looked back and saw a police car was following him* **(b)** *he never looked back* = he was very successful; *the first year after starting the business was difficult, but after that they never looked back*

☞ Definition 1

☞ Definition 2

PRACTICE
How many definitions can the following phrasal verbs have?

take off	cut in	do in	get on	go off	make up	set up

7. COMPOUND WORDS

A compound word is the main word plus another word or words. Compound words can include combinations of either nouns, verbs, adjectives or prepositions. (📖 *Compound words, p18 - 19*).

☞ **lookalike** ['lʊkəlaɪk] *noun* person who looks like someone else, especially someone famous; *they hired a Marilyn Monroe lookalike to open the new cinema*

☞ **looking glass** ['lʊkɪŋ 'glɑːs] *noun (old)* mirror; *she stared at herself in the looking-glass and saw how old she looked*

PRACTICE
Match the words on the left with the words on the right to make compound nouns.

birthday	lie	soft	trade	hard	take
junk	alarm	police	life		

over	ware	back	jacket	union	station
clock	food	party	in		

8. IDIOMS, COLLOQUIALISMS, SLANG EXPRESSIONS AND PROVERBS

- An idiom is an expression where the words do not have their literal meaning. For example, 'It's raining cats and dogs' means that it's raining heavily.
- A colloquialism is an expression which is used in common speech (they are usually informal) where the words do not have their literal meaning. For example, 'She's kicked the bucket' means that she has died.
- Slang is a popular word or phrase used by certain groups of people (eg, teenagers, students). A 'banger' is slang for an old car or a sausage.
- A proverb is a saying which teaches you something. For example, 'The early bird catches the worm' is a proverb meaning that if you decide quickly, you will succeed. Most proverbs in English have an equivalent in other languages.

Idioms, colloquialisms, slang expressions and proverbs can often be found at the end of each main entry in the dictionary. In this example (from the entry for *'look'*), there is a colloquial expression and a proverb.

Colloquialism☞ | ... *he opened the lid the box and looked inside* **(b) to look someone in the eye** = to look straight at someone in a confident way; *he didn't dare look me in the eye;* **don't look**
Proverb☞ | **a gift horse in the mouth** = don't criticize something which someone has given you for free **(c)** to appear to be; *I went to see her in hospital and she looks*

If you cannot find an expression in the main entry, look at the entries which come after it, or try looking for it under another word. You will usually find the expression in the entry for one of its key words. These key words are usually nouns, verbs or adjectives.

PRACTICE

1. What would you do if someone offered you a *fag*?
2. What does the proverb *A bird in the hand is worth two in the bush* mean?
3. If somebody is described as a *wet blanket*, what kind of person are they?
4. If you are *on cloud nine*, how do you feel?
5. Last night you *slept like a log*. Did you sleep well or badly?
6. Why should you be worried if your bank account is *in the red*?

(📖 *Pages 22 - 73*)

Review

Without looking back at the previous pages, do the following task:
In the dictionary entries below and on the next page, draw a circle around the following items.

1. Two compound nouns
2. The main word
3. Four definitions
4. A phrasal verb
5. Two derivatives
6. An idiomatic expression
7. Two grammatical functions
8. Some pronunciation symbols
9. A proverb

---

look [luk] **1** *noun* **(a)** seeing something with your eyes; *have a good look at this photograph and tell me if you recognise anyone in it; we only had time for a quick look round the town* **(b)** the way someone or something appears; *there is a French look about her clothes;* **good looks** = pleasing and beautiful appearance; *his good looks and charm attracted many women* **(c)** searching for something; *we had a good look for the ring and couldn't find it anywhere* **2** *verb* **(a)** to turn your eyes towards something; *I want you to look carefully at this photograph; look in the restaurant and see if there are any tables free; if you look out of the office window you can see our house; he opened the lid the box and looked inside* **(b)** **to look someone in the eye** = to look straight at someone in a confident way; *he didn't dare look me in the eye;* **don't look a gift horse in the mouth** = don't criticize something which someone has given you for free **(c)** to appear to be; *I went to see her in hospital and she looks worse; is he only forty? - he looks much older than that; those pies look good; it looks as if it may snow*

lookalike ['lukəlaık] *noun* person who looks like someone else, especially someone famous; *they hired a Marilyn Monroe lookalike to open the new cinema*

look back ['luk 'bæk] *verb* **(a)** to turn your head to see what is behind you; *he looked back and saw a police car was following him* **(b)** **he never looked back** = he was very successful; *the first year after starting the business was difficult, but after that they never looked back*

looking glass ['lukɪŋ 'glɑːs] *noun* (old) mirror; *she stared at herself in the looking-glass and saw how old she looked*

---

complete [kəm'pliːt] **1** *adjective* with all its parts; *he has a complete set of the new stamps; we have to study the complete works of Shakespeare* **2** *verb* **(a)** to finish; *the builders completed the whole job in two days* **(b)** to fill in a form; *when you have completed the application form, send it to us in the envelope provided*

completely [kʌm'pliːtli] *adverb* totally; *the town was completely destroyed in the earthquake; I completely forgot about my dentist's appointment*

completion [kəm'pliːʃn] *noun* act of finishing; *the bridge is nearing completion;* **completion of a contract** = signing of a contract

---

Other dictionary features

10. PLURAL FORMS.

When a noun changes from singular to plural, we usually add an *s* (cat - cats, television - televisions). Sometimes, however, we may add extra letters, change the letters or not change the word at all. The dictionary shows this. The dictionary also provides extra information based on the main word.

information ☞

sheep [ʃiːp] *noun* common farm animal, which gives wool and meat; *a flock of sheep; the sheep are in the field; see also* BLACK SHEEP (NOTE: no plural: **one sheep, ten sheep**. A female is a **ewe**, a male is a **ram**, and the young are **lambs**. Note also that the meat from a **sheep** is called **lamb**, or sometimes **mutton**)

☞ plural form

PRACTICE.

What are the plural forms of the following words?

crisis   wife   fish   potato   tomato   knife   phenomenon   bacterium   child   man   woman
patch   scarf   half   wolf

11. GRAMMATICAL, CULTURAL AND OTHER BACKGROUND INFORMATION

Some entries in the dictionary are followed by information which you may find useful or interesting. Some of this information tells you about habits, traditions, people, places and institutions in the United Kingdom.

juror [ˈdʒʊərə] *noun* member of a jury; *when I was a juror, the case lasted two weeks*

☞

COMMENT: jurors are selected from people on the register of electors who are aged between 18 and 65 years old. Various categories of people cannot be selected to serve on juries: barristers, solicitors, judges, doctors and Members of Parliament, among others.

PRACTICE (A)

Answer these questions:

1.	Who are the most important judges in Britain?
2.	How do you play cricket?
3.	What is the difference between a British pepperpot and an American pepperpot?
4.	Do British friends usually shake hands when they meet?
5.	What is a 'full English breakfast'?
6.	What do British people remember on November 5th?
7.	Do British people have to carry ID cards?
8.	What would you find inside a Christmas cracker?

PRACTICE (B)

Answer these questions:

1.	What is a *superlative* and how is it formed?
2.	What is an *auxiliary verb* and how many are there in English?
3.	When do we use *apostrophes*?
4.	What is a *modal verb* and how many are there in English?

12. BRITISH AND AMERICAN ENGLISH

If there is a difference between a word in British-English and a word in American-English, the dictionary will show this. (*Pages 26 - 27*)

> **chemist** ['kemɪst] *noun* **(a)** person who sells medicines and also prepares them; *ask the chemist to give you something for indigestion;* **the chemist's** = shop where you can buy medicine, toothpaste, soap, etc.; *go to the chemist's and get me some cough medicine* (NOTE: in American English this is usually a **drugstore** *or* **pharmacy**)   **(b)** scientist who studies chemical substances; *he works as a chemist in a nuclear laboratory*

PRACTICE

Which of these words are British-English and which are American-English?

> candy   cupboard   elevator   janitor   faucet   wallet   store   expressway

13. IRREGULAR VERBS AND OTHER INFORMATION

You will find a list of irregular verbs in the supplement at the back of your dictionary. You will also find other information which you may find useful.

PRACTICE

Answer these questions:

1.	What is the past simple and past participle form of the verb *spin*?
2.	What are the past simple and past participle forms of *overdo*?
3.	What do the past simple and past participle forms of *burn*, *dream*, *dwell* and *learn* all have in common?
4.	How do you say the telephone number *0171-921-3567*?
5.	How do you say *£27.36*?
6.	How do you say the year *1998*?
7.	How do you say the year *2000*?
8.	How do you say the date *2.1.98* in (a) Britain (b) the USA
9.	If it is midday in London, what time is it in: (a) Cairo (b) Athens (c) Singapore?
10.	What is the international telephone code for the United Kingdom?
11.	What is the international telephone code for Spain?

Nouns formed from verbs and adjectives ~
Abstract nouns

PROFILE
A. A lot of verbs and adjectives can be changed to nouns by the addition of extra letters (eg, *-ment*, *-ion*, *-ation*) or by changing other features of the word.

- In most cases, the nouns are *abstract*. This means that we cannot usually touch, see, feel, hear or smell them.
- The opposite of an abstract noun is a concrete noun. This is something that we can touch, see, feel, hear or smell.
- Most, but not all, abstract nouns are uncountable. This means that we cannot count them and usually we cannot use the words *a* or *an* before them.
- Some nouns formed from verbs or adjectives can be either abstract or concrete (eg, *survive = survival* (abstract) - continuing to exist - **or** *survivor* (concrete) - a person who is still alive after an accident.
- Most abstract nouns end with *-ment*, *-ion*, *-ation*, *-ness*, *-ity* or *-ence*.

B. *Dictionary practice*
1. Look up the verb *argue* in your dictionary
2. What is the noun for argue?
3. Which letters does the noun end with?
4. What else do you notice about the spelling?

NOUNS FORMED FROM VERBS
Look at the verbs in the box, use your dictionary to find the nouns that are derived from them and put them into the table on the next page with their appropriate form. Be careful with your spelling! There are some examples to help you.

astonish	obey	laugh	persist	arrive
qualify	repeat	embarrass	announce	arrange
treat	admire	vary	survive	assist
die	lose	please	break	form
satisfy	permit	sign	believe	choose
be born	resist	approve	organize	argue
develop	amaze	discuss	pronounce	perform
insist	behave	complain	succeed	receive
expect	discover	fail	prove	prefer
disappear	cancel	hesitate	complete	excite
discover				

-ment	-ion	-ation	Others
excitement	discussion	expectation	preference

PRACTICE

Complete each of these sentences with a suitable abstract noun. The first letter of each word has been given.

1. The next p............... will begin at 8 o'clock.
2. The children are always in a state of e.............. before the holiday.
3. I tried to improve my p.............. by listening to British people.
4. She gave b.............. to a baby boy last night.
5. Does she have the right q............... for the job?
6. She had a terrible a............... with her boss and resigned a few days later.
7. Much to my e.............. I arrived an hour late. Of course, I went bright red!
8. Alexander Fleming is credited with the d............... of penicillin.
9. To my great a............... they paid the bill in full.
10. We were all puzzled by the sudden d............... of our guide; one moment he was with us, the next moment we couldn't see him anywhere.

NOUNS FORMED FROM ADJECTIVES

Look at the adjectives in the box on the next page, find the nouns that are derived from them and put them into the table with their appropriate form. Use your dictionary to find out the meanings of any words you don't understand. Be careful with your spelling! There are some examples to help you.

relevant	patient	pure	responsible	thirsty
brave	accurate	selfish	wide	long
bored	stupid	confident	intelligent	deep
loyal	popular	valid	proud	high
happy	similar	mature	anxious	honest
realistic	ill	probable	hungry	inferior
violent	rare	angry	equal	reliable
pessimistic	foolish	insolent	necessary	true
hot	sympathetic	certain	superior	
just	warm	lonely	safe	
optimistic	white	possible	strong	

-ity	-ence	-ness	Others
maturity	violence	tidiness	heat

PRACTICE

Complete each of these sentences with a suitable abstract noun. The first letter of each word has been given.

1. The h........ of the sun made the ice cream melt.
2. She hasn't got the s........ to lift the suitcase.
3. Do you think he's telling the t........?
4. All acts of v........ , for example by terrorists, must be punished.
5. There are children dying of h........ in some countries in Africa.
6. I don't have the p........ to wait that long.
7. He won a medal for b........ .
8. I admire him for his h........ in saying the job was too difficult for him.
9. A feeling of h........ came over her as he spoke.
10. She developed a serious i............... and was sent to hospital.

Compound words

PROFILE

A. A compound word is a word (eg a noun, a verb, a preposition or an adjective) plus another word which, when combined, make another noun or adjective.

- Some compound words can be written as one word. eg, videorecorder.
- Some compound words can be joined using a hyphen (-). eg, half-brother.
- Some compound words must be written as two words. eg, television set.

There are no rules to tell us how a compound word should be written, although compound adjectives are often written with a hyphen.

B. *Dictionary practice*
1. Look up the word *birthday* in your dictionary.
2. How many compound words are there?
3. Are these written as (a) one word, (b) with a hyphen or (c) two words.
4. Look up the word *half* in your dictionary.
5. How many compound words are there?
6. Are these written as (a) one word, (b) with a hyphen or (c) two words.
7. Look up the word *trade* in your dictionary.
8. How many compound words are there?
9. How many can be written (a) as one word, (b) with a hyphen and (c) as two words?

1. COMPOUND NOUNS.

Join one word on the left with one word on the right to make compound nouns. In some cases, more than one combination is possible.

| food home fairy moon book hair |
| income air tooth traffic football race |
| table parking water time stamp airline |
| sun question shoe |

| pollution boots lights relations pilot |
| laces light tax glasses meter collection |
| mark table basin story poisoning paste |
| dryer case tennis work |

Use the compound nouns to complete the following sentences:

1. The children enjoyed listening to the _____
2. Wait for the _____ to turn green before continuing.
3. These plants need lots of water and plenty of _____.
4. _____ is caused by cars and industry.
5. _____ in the city are very bad. There are often fights between black and white youths.
6. The more money you earn, the more _____ you have to pay.
7. He ate some bad fish and now he's in bed with _____ .
8. Do your _____ up or you'll trip over.
9. Don't forget to put some money in the _____ or you'll get a ticket.
10. When does our train leave? Why don't you check the _____ .

2. COMPOUND ADJECTIVES

Join one word on the left with one word on the right to make compound adjectives.

| world- short- sun- well- run- absent- |
| fair- hard- eye- hand- three- |

| haired star made catching down off |
| minded up sighted tanned famous |

Use the compound adjectives to complete the following sentences.

1. We stayed in a _____ hotel.
2. Mel Gibson is a _____ actor.
3. After his holiday in Spain he had a _____ face.
4. I can't see very clearly. I'm a bit _____ .
5. The tennis racket broke soon after I bought it. It wasn't very _____ .
6. She was wearing an _____ dress.
7. All these items are _____ by skilled craftsmen.
8. I feel a bit _____. I should take more vitamins.
9. My wife comes from a _____ family; they've always had more money than my family.
10. My grandfather's becoming very _____ . He went to the library in his slippers.

Based on the *English Dictionary for Students*, ISBN 1-901659-06-2

Adjectives formed from verbs

PROFILE

A. A lot of verbs can be changed to adjectives by the addition of a suffix (eg, -able, -ous, -ful) to the end of the word.

- In verbs which end with -y, the y either changes to an i or is dropped altogether.
- Some other verbs must have other letters added in addition to the suffix.
- Some verbs can have more than one adjective form.
- In some verbs which end with -e, the e is replaced with an i or dropped altogether (eg, bore - boring).

B. *Dictionary practice*

Look up the words below in your dictionary and put them into the correct space in the table, depending on their ending. Two of them can go in more than one space on the table (the meaning changes in both cases).

frighten   continue   act   admire   use

-ive	-al	-ous	-able	-ing	-ful	-ed

Complete the following sentences with an adjective formed from the verb in **bold**.

1. My grandmother is still very _____ at the age of 88. **act**
2. Her work is entirely _____ . **admire**
3. We spent a very _____ weekend by the sea. **agree**
4. She wrote us an _____ letter. **apologize**
5. I don't want to watch that _____ television programme. **bore**
6. I'm _____. Let's go out to the club. **bore**
7. Be _____ not to make any noise, the baby is asleep. **care**
8. Judged by last year's performance, it is a _____ success. **compare**
9. He's very _____ and loves playing sports. **compete**
10. She made some _____ suggestions for improving the shop. **construct**
11. The computer has given us _____ problems since we bought it. **continue**
12. She's been in _____ pain for three days. **continue**
13. He's a _____ child, always full of ideas. **create**
14. He was nervous, but tried to sound _____ . **decide**
15. People living in small villages need a _____ bus service. **depend**
16. She had a _____ expression on her face. **doubt**
17. He's a very _____ child and often has headaches. **excite**
18. The news about the house is very _____ . **excite**
19. She's _____ at the thought of going on holiday. **excite**
20. We are _____ that the company will accept our offer. **hope**
21. Any exercise is _____ to sitting around doing nothing. **prefer**
22. She was hardly _____ when she came out of prison. **recognize**
23. It was very _____ to see them getting on so well. **satisfy**
24. We became _____ when we found out that she knew about the deal. **suspect**
25. She's a very _____ person to have in the office. **use**
26. The weather can be very _____ on the coast. **vary**

© Peter Collin Publishing, 1999
Based on the *English Dictionary for Students*, ISBN 1-901659-06-2

Opposites of adjectives

PROFILE

A. A lot of adjectives can be made into their opposite form by the addition of a prefix (eg, un-, in-, dis- il-) to the beginning of the word.

- Unfortunately, there are very few rules to tell you which adjectives use which prefixes. You have to learn each one individually.
- The most common prefix is *un-*
- The main exception to this are adjectives which end with *-ful* (eg, thoughtful, useful, careful). These are made into opposites by replacing *-ful* with the suffix *-less* (eg, thoughtless, useless, careless).
- The addition of the prefix does not change the pronunciation of the original word.
- When using your dictionary to look up the opposite form of an adjective, you will need to look under the entries for one of the following prefixes: *dis- in- ir- un- il- im-*
- If you cannot find an opposite form under these entries, the opposite of the adjective is probably a different word altogether (📖 *Opposites, page 59*)
- Some adjectives can be made into opposites by the addition of a prefix *or* by the use of another word (eg, *correct = incorrect* or *wrong*)

B. *Dictionary practice*

Use your dictionary to check whether the adjectives in bold are <u>correct</u> or <u>incorrect</u>.

1. We had an **unagreeable** meeting with the tax inspectors.
2. This puzzle is **incomplete** - there's a piece missing.
3. Having to leave at 5.30 in the morning is **unacceptable**.
4. The house is **irattractive** from the outside, but the inside is quite extraordinary.
5. It's **imlogical** to increase prices when sales are falling.
6. It's **illegal** to serve alcohol to people under 16.

Put the adjectives below into the correct space in the table on the next page depending on the prefix they use to become opposites.

qualified	rational	avoidable	complete	mortal	pure	accurate	adequate	conscious

qualified   rational   avoidable   complete   mortal   pure   accurate   adequate   conscious
moral   legal   acceptable   attractive   possible   legitimate   regular   literate   fair   curable
advantaged   resolute   satisfied   responsible   convincing   even   married   welcome
comfortable   fashionable   limited   logical   mature   mobile   patient   perfect
agreeable   certain   replaceable   contented   honest   proper   inclined   competent
obedient   relevant   believable   personal   resistible   correct

dis-	il-	im-	in-	ir-	un-

Based on the *English Dictionary for Students*, ISBN 1-901659-06-2

Complete these sentences with a word from the grid.

1. We can't accept the terms of the contract. They are completely _____ .
2. We'll never be able to replace the old photographs which were stolen. They are _____ .
3. Sally has so much work to do. It's _____ to expect her to do all the housework while her sisters don't lift a finger to help.
4. He's always in a hurry and gets very _____ with anyone who works slowly.
5. It's _____ to serve alcohol to people under sixteen. If you do, you'll be breaking the law.
6. This Internet account provides you with _____ e-mail addresses; you can have as many as you like.
7. I've never seen such a group of _____ little children. They never do anything I tell them to.
8. I wish she would grow up and stop being so _____. She's an adult, not a child.
9. A lot of children in this area can't read or write, but with so few schools or teachers it is not surprising that so many of them are _____ .
10. Their plans are still _____ - they're not sure whether to stay in London or get a job abroad.
11. There aren't many facilities for poor people in this town. It's a very _____ area.
12. I can't resist chocolate cake, I find it completely _____ .
13. She's been _____ since the accident two days ago and isn't aware of what has happened.
14. I've never come across a _____ policeman, although there are always stories in the papers telling us that the police can't be trusted.
15. It was _____ of her to leave the two children at home while she went on holiday. She often does reckless and senseless things like that.

© Peter Collin Publishing, 1999
Based on the *English Dictionary for Students*, ISBN 1-901659-06-2

Opposites of verbs

PROFILE

A. Some verbs can be made into their opposite form by the addition of a prefix (eg, dis- , mis-)

- Unfortunately, there are very few rules to tell you which verbs use which prefixes. You have to learn each one individually.
- Some verbs drop the first part of the word before the prefix is added (eg, *encourage* becomes *discourage*)
- The addition of the prefix does not change the pronunciation of the original word.
- When using your dictionary to look up the opposite form of a verb, you should look under the entries for the following prefixes: *dis- mis- un-*
- If you cannot find an opposite form under these entries, the opposite of the verb is probably a different word altogether (📖 *Opposites, page 59*)

B. *Dictionary practice*

Use your dictionary to check whether the verbs in bold are correct or incorrect.

1. He hit the ball hard and it **misappeared** into the bushes.
2. Our aims and intentions have been **disrepresented** by the press.
3. He **misfastened** his belt and tucked his shirt into his trousers.

Complete these sentences with the opposite form of one of the verbs in the box. Not all of the words are needed. You will need to change the form of the verb in several cases.

use	agree	like	behave	place	obey	understand	continue	cover	fold	load
connect	prove	qualify	wrap	pack	lock	pronounce	approve	trust	please	

1. If anyone _____, they will be sent home immediately.
2. I've just come back from Canada and I'm still _____ my suitcases.
3. Here's a photo of our little girl _____ her Christmas presents.
4. She's a very obedient young lady. She would never _____ her parents.
5. She _____ the money which she had been given. She was supposed to use it to pay for her education, but bought a sports car instead.
6. The head teacher _____ of members of staff wearing jeans to school, and insists that they dress smartly at all times.
7. German speakers of English sometimes _____ 'th' as 'z'.
8. His statement to the police said that he was nowhere near the bank, but they managed to _____ this.
9. I _____ anyone who wears green shoes but I can't tell you why.
10. I can't _____ the car door. I think I've got the wrong key.
11. After the accident he was fined £1,000 and _____ from driving for two years.
12. She _____ the tablecloth and put it on the table.
13. We don't sell *Sonic* cameras any longer. We have _____ that line.
14. I seem to have _____ my keys. I can't find them anywhere.
15. If you refuse to pay your gas bill, you will be _____ .

Nouns formed from nouns and verbs

PROFILE

- Some nouns can be formed by taking another noun or verb and either <u>adding letters</u>, <u>removing letters</u> or a <u>combination of both</u>. This is especially common when we are talking about jobs and occupations (for example: *sail - sailor*)
- There are no rules which tell you how each word changes. You must learn each one individually.
- The removal or addition of letters occasionally changes the pronunciation of parts of the original word.

Use the instructions on the right to change the words on the left to nouns in order to give the names of the people who do those things. Some of the instructions on the right can be used more than once.

| *Example*: | **crime** : | **minus 1 letter plus** *-inal* | = | **criminal** |

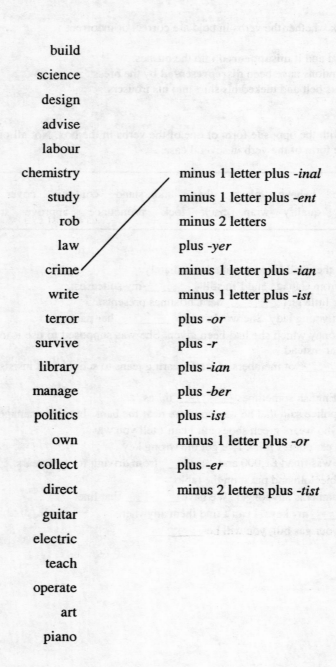

build	
science	
design	
advise	
labour	
chemistry	minus 1 letter plus *-inal*
study	minus 1 letter plus *-ent*
rob	minus 2 letters
law	plus *-yer*
crime	minus 1 letter plus *-ian*
write	minus 1 letter plus *-ist*
terror	plus *-or*
survive	plus *-r*
library	plus *-ian*
manage	plus *-ber*
politics	plus *-ist*
own	minus 1 letter plus *-or*
collect	plus *-er*
direct	minus 2 letters plus *-tist*
guitar	
electric	
teach	
operate	
art	
piano	

© Peter Collin Publishing, 1999
Based on the *English Dictionary for Students*, ISBN 1-901659-06-2

Modified words

PROFILE

On pages 17 - 19, you looked at how verbs and adjectives could be made into opposites by adding on other letters.

- It is also possible to add other letters (prefixes) to change, or *modify*, the main meaning of a verb, noun or adjective without making it into an opposite (eg, *pay - overpay - underpay*)
- The prefixes we use to do this are:
  For verbs: *over- , under- , pre-, fore-*
  For adjectives: *over- , under- , pre- , fore- , pro- , anti- .*
  For nouns: *pre- , post- , anti- , pro- , under-*

Complete the sentences below with a combination of a prefix from box A and a verb or adjective from box B.

A.				
anti-	over-	anti-	under-	pro-
fore-	fore-	under-	pre-	fore-
post-	fore-	under-	anti-	over-

B.					
mined	see	warned	social	armed	graduates
estimated	due	estimate	European	clockwise	
Christmas	holiday	climax			

1. After weeks·of preparation, it was a bit of an _____ when we discovered we couldn't leave because of the weather. We were so disappointed.

2. Do you _____ any problems with the visa? I need to know as soon as possible if we're likely to have difficulties.

3. Everyone's suffering from _____ gloom. After all that Mediterranean sun, the gloomy weather here is making us all so depressed.

4. The figure of £50,000 was a bit of an _____ . It actually cost us almost £70,000.

5. She's _____ and believes that the country should remain part of the EU.

6. He's very _____, he never goes to parties.

7. A lot of _____ are trying to get holiday jobs so that they have some spending money next term.

8. She was _____ with good advice before she went into the interview.

9. He was driving _____ round the ring road when the accident took place. If he had been going the other way, he would have been all right.

10. We were _____ of trouble by our spies and took guns to the meeting.

11. I always read my horoscope so that I can _____ what will happen to me during the week.

12. Her library books were _____ by four weeks, so she had to pay a fine.

13. Our heavy industry is being _____ by low labour costs in the Far East.

14. We had so many _____ parties that by the time the big day arrived I couldn't eat or drink another thing.

15. He _____ the amount of time needed to fit out the factory; he thought it would take ten weeks but it only took seven.

© Peter Collin Publishing, 1999
Based on the *English Dictionary for Students*, ISBN 1-901659-06-2

Abbreviations and acronyms

1. ORGANISATIONS AND PEOPLE

A. *Look at the sentences below and decide which organisation or person is being described. Choose from one of the abbreviations in the box.*

OPEC	NHS	VIP	EU	MP	CIA	CID	AA	BBC	UN	WHO	PC	FBI	UK	MEP

1. An international organization including almost all the sovereign states (☞sovereign, def 2) in the world, where member states are represented at meetings.
2. A part of (1) which aims to improve health in the world by teaching and publishing information about diseases.
3. A British national radio and television company.
4. A department of the British police which investigates serious crimes (☞crime).
5. An American government agency which organises spies (☞spy, def 1).
6. The main police agency for fighting crime in the USA.
7. An organization which links several European countries together and which is based on freedom of movement of goods, of capital (☞capital, def 1b), of people and of services.
8. A system of free doctors, nurses, hospitals and clinics, run by the British government.
9. A British organization which offers services to its members, such as insurance, emergency repairs to vehicles, etc.
10. A group of countries who produce and export oil.
11. An independent country, formed of England, Scotland, Wales and Northern Ireland.
12. A person elected to represent a constituency (☞constituency) in the British Parliament.
13. A person elected to represent a constituency in the European Parliament.
14. An ordinary member of the British police.
15. A very important person.

B. *Complete the news broadcast below with one of the abbreviations from the exercise above.*

Good evening. Here is the news.

(1)_____ s from the British Parliament, and (2)_____'s from the European Parliament have met in Strasbourg to discuss Britain's future in Europe. In a recent survey, it was revealed that most British people no longer want to be part of the (3)_____, despite the benefits which the four main freedoms have brought.

The (4)_____ has warned that tuberculosis is increasing, especially in tropical countries. The Secretary-General of the (5)_____ has offered his full support to help prevent the spread of the disease.

Despite the current world recession, (6)_____ has warned that it will shortly increase oil prices again. In a television interview with the (7)_____, the Prime Minister announced that this rise, the third this year, will have serious repercussions (☞repercussions).

The hunt is still on for international bankrobber Pinko Pallino. Detectives with the (8)_____ in London have met their American counterparts from the (9)_____ to plan a strategy to catch him.

And finally, as temperatures drop below zero again tonight, the (10)_____ have warned drivers to be especially careful on the roads. They say that you should only go out if your journey is extremely important.

That's all for now. The next news will be at 9 o'clock.

© Peter Collin Publishing, 1999
Based on the *English Dictionary for Students*, ISBN 1-901659-06-2

2. COMMON ABBREVIATIONS
Look at the following situations and choose the best answer, A, B or C.

1. You receive an invitation which has **RSVP** printed on the bottom. What should you do?
   (a) Wear your best clothes.
   (b) Reply to the invitation.
   (c) Bring something to drink with you.

2. A memo from your boss asking you to send an e-mail to another company has the abbreviation **ASAP** on it. What should you do?
   (a) Send the e-mail as soon as you can - it's important.
   (b) Show your boss the e-mail before you send it.
   (c) Give the job to someone else.

3. A letter you are reading has **PTO** written at the bottom. What should you do?
   (a) Destroy it after you have read it.
   (b) Photocopy it and give copies to your friends / colleagues.
   (c) Turn the page over as the letter is continued on the back.

4. An advertisement for a car has "£4,000 **o.n.o.**" on it. What does this mean?
   (a) The seller will exchange the car for another one.
   (b) The seller wants you to pay a minimum of £4,000.
   (c) The seller will accept a price slightly lower than £4,000.

5. A television you are buying has a price label saying "£750 including **VAT**". How much will you have to pay for the television?
   (a) More than £750
   (b) Less than £750
   (c) £750 exactly

6. You are looking for a flat in the newspaper. An advertisement for a flat you are interested in has the abbreviation **n/s**. What does this mean?
   (a) The flat can't be rented by students.
   (b) The flat is near a station.
   (c) The flat can only be rented by a non-smoker.

7. Where are you likely to see the abbreviation **PS**?
   (a) Outside a police station.
   (b) At the end of a letter.
   (c) Outside a private school.

8. What does the abbreviation **eg** mean?
   (a) please note
   (b) at the end
   (c) for example

© Peter Collin Publishing, 1999
Based on the *English Dictionary for Students*, ISBN 1-901659-06-2

Accommodation

1. VERBS

*Rearrange the words in **bold** and write them in the grid on the right. The first letter of each word has been underlined. When you have finished, you will find another word which means 'to make a building like new again' in the shaded vertical strip*

1. I really think we should **roce̲deta** the kitchen. What colour do you think would be best?
2. We need to **te̲rn** a flat in the middle of town, but I think they're quite expensive.
3. The landlord (☞landlord, def a) is going to **ne̲texd** the lease (☞lease, def 1a) on our flat.
4. The council want to **me̲doshli** our apartment block as they think it's dangerous.
5. I think the landlord is going to **ti̲cve** us soon; he's says we make too much noise.
6. We plan to **se̲ale** our spare offices to an American company.
7. The flat is to **t̲le** at £1,000 per month.
8. They've bought a new house and are going to **me̲ov ni̲** next week.

2. NOUNS AND ADJECTIVES

A. *Read the descriptions 1 - 14 and decide which type of accommodation is being described in each one. Use your dictionary to look up the meanings of the adjectives in **bold**.*

detached house	semi-detached house	terraced house	mansion	palace	castle	bungalow
cottage	caravan	prison cell	hospital ward	barracks	houseboat	flat

1. It's quite an old house, and the walls are paper-thin, so we can hear everything the neighbours on both sides are doing.	6. It's lovely out here in the countryside and we try to spend as much time here as possible. It's quite a little house, but very **cosy**, of course.
2. There are three of us in here and it's really **claustrophobic**, especially as we can't open the window and the door is locked all the time.	7. It's a very large, **spacious** house with a long drive, beautiful gardens and a view over the golf course. There are fifteen bedrooms, although we don't use them all of course!
3. The patients on either side of me are really nice, which is good because otherwise this place is really **depressing**. I hope I get well soon.	8. Although we live in the city, our house stands alone in its own garden. This means that we don't get any noise from the neighbours on either side.
4. Towers and turrets, bastions and battlements. Mist on the moat and dragons under the drawbridge. This place is **awe-inspiring**.	9. Our next door neighbour likes to play loud music at night, so we moved the bedroom to the other side of the house where there aren't any neighbours directly next door.
5. It's a bit **cramped**, but the great advantage is that, when we get fed up with one place, we just attach it to the back of the car and move on.	10. I'm not sure who lives there now, but at one time it was the residence of King George III. It's very **grandiose**; 120 bedrooms and almost 600 hectares (☞hectare) of land.
11. My grandparents bought it last year. It only has one floor, so they don't have to worry about climbing the stairs.	13. The block where we live is next to the underground station. It's smaller than our old house, of course, but we have a great view from the 8th floor.
12. It's moored (☞moor, def 2) on the River Thames near London. It's very peaceful, apart from the noise from the ducks and geese.	14. There are fifteen of us in here, but the sergeant-major makes sure we keep it tidy. If we don't, we get extra guard-duty!

© Peter Collin Publishing, 1999
Based on the *English Dictionary for Students*, ISBN 1-901659-06-2

B. *Rearrange these words so that they are in order, from the highest part of the house to the lowest part. The highest part and the lowest part have already been done.*

Highest

| ground floor |
| second floor |
| television aerial |
| first floor |
| cellar |
| chimney |
| roof |
| roof gutter |
| attic |

| television aerial |
| |
| |
| |
| |
| |
| |
| |
| cellar |

Lowest

3. IDIOMS, COLLOQUIALISMS AND OTHER EXPRESSIONS
Look at the following sentences and decide whether the explanations which follow them are TRUE or FALSE.

1. The hotel is a real **home from home**.
    The hotel is not very comfortable. TRUE / FALSE

2. He lay down on the sofa, opened a bottle of beer and **made himself at home**.
    He behaved differently from the way he did in his own house. TRUE / FALSE

3. His new job is **nothing to write home about**.
    His new job is not very exciting or special. TRUE / FALSE

4. The pub serves **homely** food.
    The food in the pub is not very good. TRUE / FALSE

5. I had to tell her a few **home truths**.
    I had to tell her some unpleasant facts about her. TRUE / FALSE

6. Cheer up, we're in the **home straight** now!
    We've been working on a long project and have almost finished it. TRUE / FALSE

7. James lives in **cardboard city**.
    James lives in a very comfortable house. TRUE / FALSE

8. The staff in the hotel were very **accommodating**.
    The staff in the hotel were very helpful. TRUE / FALSE

9. Caron is my **flat-mate**.
    Caron lives in the flat next door to mine. TRUE / FALSE

British and American English

English is spoken as a first language by 415 million people world-wide, and by a further 800 million people as a second language. While English grammar and spelling are almost universal, there are quite a lot of differences in the vocabulary of different regions. One of the biggest differences is between the English which is spoken in the United Kingdom, and the English which is spoken in the United States.

If you are doing a British examination (eg, the First Certificate), it is acceptable to use American English, but you should use it consistently (☞consistently).

1. SPELLING
There are only a few differences in spelling between British and American English. Use your dictionary to find out how the following words are spelt in American English.

British English	American English
centre	
traveller	
colour	
dialogue	

Can you think of any other words which follow the same rules?

2. VOCABULARY
A. *Look at the following pairs of conversations. Each pair is identical, except one uses British-English words and one uses American-English words. These are shown in **bold**. Decide which conversation is British and which is American English. Then use your dictionary to check your answers.*

1A. "I must go to the **drugstore** to get some **diapers**. Have you seen my **billfold**?"
   "I think you put it in the pocket of your new **pants**. They're hanging up in the **closet** under the stairs."

1B. "I must go to the **chemist's** to get some **nappies**. Have you seen my **wallet**?"
   "I think you put it in the pocket of your new **trousers**. They're hanging up in the **cupboard** under the stairs"

2A. "Let's go to the **cinema** tonight. It's been ages since I saw a good **film**."
   "We can't. The **car**'s out of **petrol**."
   "No problem. We can take the **tube**. Have you got enough money?"
   "I'm not sure. Where's my **handbag**? I can't find it **anywhere**. Oh no! I think I left it in the **off-licence** earlier."

2B. "Let's go to the **movies** tonight. It's been ages since I saw a good **movie**."
   "We can't. The **automobile**'s out of **gas**."
   "No problem. We can take the **subway**. Have you got enough money?"
   "I'm not sure. Where's my **purse**? I can't find it **anyplace**. Oh no! I think I left it in the **liquor store** earlier."

3A. "Could you go to the **store**? We need some **cookies**, **chips** and **candy** for the children's' party."
   "OK. I've only got a large **bill**, though. Have you got anything smaller?"
   "No I haven't. Why don't you ask the **neighbor**?"
   "Which one?"
   "Mrs Simpson. She lives in the **apartment** on the **first** floor. Take the **elevator**. If she's not in, ask the **janitor**."

3B. "Could you go to the **shop**? We need some **biscuits**, **crisps** and **sweets** for the children's' party."
   "OK. I've only got a large **note**, though. Have you got anything smaller?"
   "No, I haven't. Why don't you ask the **neighbour**?"
   "Which one?"
   "Mrs Simpson. She lives in the **flat** on the **ground** floor. Take the **lift**. If she's not in, ask the **caretaker**."

© Peter Collin Publishing, 1999
Based on the *English Dictionary for Students*, ISBN 1-901659-06-2

4A.	"I'm sending a birthday card to Joy. Do you know her **postcode**?"
	"Here it is. Are you going to **post** it today?"
	"Actually, I was hoping you would take it to the **postbox** for me."
4B.	"I'm sending a birthday card to Joy. Do you know her **zip code**?"
	"Here it is. Are you going to **mail** it today?"
	"Actually, I was hoping you would take it to the **mailbox** for me."

B. *Replace one of the British-English words in the following sentences with an American-English word from the box.*

garbage can   fall   yard   check   expressway   play hookey   vacation   intermission   attorney
railroad   faucet   eraser   raise   rest room   stove   sidewalk

1.   He washed his hands under the tap in the kitchen.
2.   If you are arrested, you have the right to speak to your lawyer.
3.   He used a rubber to try to rub out what he had written.
4.   You will get there faster if you take the motorway.
5.   In autumn, the leaves turn brown.
6.   She put the rest of the dinner in the dustbin.
7.   There will be a short interval, during which the stage will be cleared.
8.   The railway station is in the centre of town.
9.   If I don't get a rise soon, I'll start looking for another job.
10.   The ladies' toilet is at the end of the corridor.
11.   Be careful if you go for a walk. The pavement is covered with ice.
12.   We have a fridge, a dishwasher and a gas cooker in the kitchen.
13.   When are you planning to go on holiday?
14.   Your sister's outside, sitting in the garden.
15.   Leonard always gets bad grades because he likes to play truant from school.
16.   Ask the waiter for the bill.

Cars and driving

1. NOUNS
A. *Name the parts of the car indicated in the two pictures using the words in the box.*

THE EXTERIOR

headlights	windscreen	mirrors	bumper	bonnet	boot	tyre	indicators	radiator grille
		aerial	number plate					

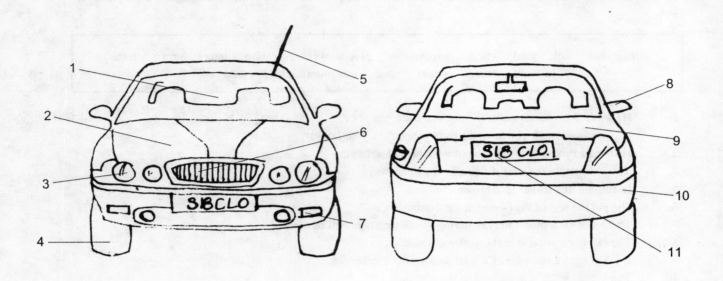

THE INTERIOR

steering wheel	speedometer	brake pedal	handbrake	glove compartment	clutch pedal	accelerator
	gear lever	tax disk	horn	petrol gauge	mirror	

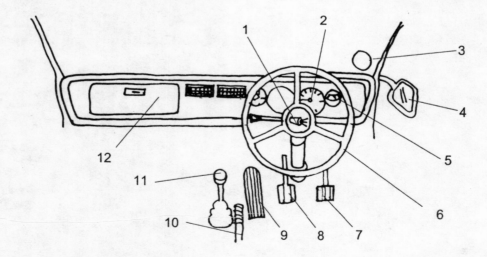

B. *Use your dictionary to find the difference between the following groups of words.*

1. a saloon, a hatchback and an estate
2. a lorry, a van and a truck
3. a coach, a bus and a minibus
4. a main road and a slip road
5. a crossroads, a T-junction and a fork
6. a highway and a motorway

7. the central reservation and the hard shoulder
8. traffic lights and a traffic island
9. a zebra crossing and a pelican crossing
10. a tunnel and a flyover

2. VERBS
Complete the story below with an appropriate word or expression from the box.

crashed	accelerated	indicate	reverse	overtake	smashed	skidded	started up	braked	fasten
swerve	adjust	sounded	check	stalled	release	pulled away			

I've just finished my driving test and I think it went quite well. OK, so I made a few mistakes, but nothing too serious. For example, I forgot to 1._____ the mirrors, with the result that I couldn't see anything behind me. Then, when I 2._____ the car, I forgot that I had left it in first gear, so I 3._____. Oh, and I forgot to 4._____ my seatbelt. And 5._____ the handbrake. When I eventually 6._____ from the side of the road, I forgot to 7._____ my mirrors; the driver of the car that almost 8._____ into me as a result 9._____ his horn and shouted something at me, but I didn't hear what. I nearly went through a red light, but saw it at the last second and tried to stop. Unfortunately, I lost control and my car 10._____ across to the other side of the road - fortunately, the cars coming in the opposite direction managed to 11._____ out of the way. At one point, I 12._____ when I should have 13._____, so instead of stopping, the car just went faster! Fortunately, the police car that I 14._____ into the back of wasn't badly damaged and the policeman driving it didn't shout at me too loudly. At another time I had to 15._____ somebody who was driving a bit slowly, but I forgot to 16._____, so the drivers behind me had no idea what I was going to do. Finally, I managed to 17._____ into a wall which I couldn't see behind me. I don't know if I've passed yet, because the examiner is still being treated for shock (☞shock, def 1b) in the local hòspital.

3. IDIOMS, COLLOQUIALISMS AND OTHER EXPRESSIONS
<u>*The worst driver in the world?*</u> *Read the following story and use your dictionary to look up the meanings of the words and expressions in* **bold**.

My brother Ted must be the world's worst driver. It started when he was young and used to go for **joyrides**, causing **pile-ups** which resulted in **traffic jams** and **gridlocks** for other drivers. As a young adult, he was a real boy **racer**, **putting his foot down**, driving **like the clappers** and then **jamming on the brakes**. I reckon he must have **written off** at least six of the **bangers** he used to drive. He's still a real **road hog**, **tailgating** other cars and getting involved in **road rage** incidents. He's offered to **give me a lift** home tonight, but to be honest, I'd rather **thumb a lift**. He's **picking me up** in a few minutes; maybe I'd better have **one for the road**. At least it's **rush hour** and the roads will be **chock-a-block** so he won't be able to drive too fast! Honestly - sometimes he **drives me round the bend**!

Clothes

1. VERBS

Look at the sentences below and fill in the gaps using the appropriate word or expression from A, B or C.

1. It takes him ages every morning to get up, _____, and have breakfast.
    A. put on   B. wear   C. get dressed

2. You've got an important interview today. Don't forget to _____ a tie.
    A. get dressed   B. try on   C. put on

3. What dress are you going to _____ to the party?
    A. wear   B. get dressed   C. try on

4. Did you _____ the shoes in the shop before you bought them?
    A. wear   B. try on   C. fit

5. These shoes don't _____ me - they're a size too small.
    A. fit   B. measure   C. suit

6. Green clothes usually _____ people with red hair.
    A. fit   B. suit   C. match

7. Your yellow trousers don't _____ your bright green shirt.
    A. fit   B. measure   C. match

8. He's _____ his coat - it's too small for him now.
    A. grown into   B. grown out of   C. grown up

9. Walking across the USA, he _____ three pairs of boots.
    A. wore off   B. wore out   C. wore on

10. The doctor asked the patient to _____.
    A. undress   B. undo   C. untie

11. Can you _____ the zip (☞zip, def 1) at the back of my dress?
    A. do up   B. tie up   C. put on

12. Would you mind _____ my shirt please?
    A. creasing   B. ironing   C. squashing

2. NOUNS AND ADJECTIVES

A. Read the texts below and write the names of the people next to the appropriate items of clothing on the next page.

At a party.
That's Jim over there by the door. Can you see him? He's wearing jeans and trainers, a striped shirt and a black waistcoat.

At a fashion show.
Miranda is wearing a stunning outfit by designer Jean-Claude Cliché. Of course, many people would say that high heels, a tartan skirt, a blouse with a floral pattern and a spotted silk scarf don't match.

At the office.
Mr Johnson always wears plain trousers, a plain shirt and a jacket.

At home.
Jenny, our eldest daughter, hangs around the house in an old pleated skirt, a sweatshirt and a pair of her granny's old slippers.

On the beach.
Bob is wearing a baggy pair of shorts with a horrible floral pattern, held up with a belt, a striped T-shirt, a pair of sandals with long black socks, and a cap to protect his head from the sun. He looks a sight!

A parent's advice on a cold day.
Make sure you wear warm clothes, Tony. You'll need a thick jumper, your wellingtons, those corduroys and your brother's old overcoat. Oh, and don't forget your scarf - the checked woollen one - and your mittens.

Read the texts on the previous page and write the names of the people next to the appropriate items of clothing.

1) . . . .   2) . . . .   3) . . . .   4) . . . .   5) . . . .   6) . . . .

7) . . . .   8) . . . .   9) . . . .   10) . . . .   11) . . . .

12) . . . . . .   13) . . . . . .   14) . . . . . .   15) . . . . . .   16) . . . . . .

17) . . . . . .   18) . . . . . .   19) . . . . . .   20) . . . . . .   21) . . . . . .

B. *Match the items in the box with their definitions 1 - 8 below.*

cuff   lace   seam   sleeve   collar   pocket   buckle   button

1.   a metal fastener for a strap, usually found on a belt.
2.   part of a piece of clothing which covers your arm.
3.   a little bag sewn into the inside of a coat, etc, in which you can keep your handkerchief, keys, etc.
4.   little round disc for fastening clothes.
5.   line where two pieces of cloth are attached together.
6.   thin strip of leather, cord, etc, for tying up a shoe.
7.   part of a shirt, coat, dress, etc, which goes round your neck.
8.   end of (2) round the wrist.

3. IDIOMS, COLLOQUIALISMS AND OTHER EXPRESSIONS
The following story uses expressions involving items of clothing. Replace them using an entry from the box.

secretly   sacked him (☞sack, def 2a)   nonsense (☞nonsense)   had a plan which he was keeping secret   try to do better   place   admire   on a small amount of money   be quiet   wearing his very best clothes   secret hit her hard   worked closely

Bert had never **been hand in glove** with Mrs Jameson, our boss. One day, Mrs Jameson told him he had to **pull his socks up**. Bert told her to **belt up** and threatened to **give her a sock** in the jaw (☞jaw). She **gave him the boot** and I had to step into his **shoes**. The next day, Bert came to the office **dressed up to the nines**. He told Mrs Jameson he didn't want to be without a job and live **on a shoestring**. He said he **was keeping something up his sleeve** which he could use against the company, but would keep it **under his hat** if she gave him his job back. Mrs Jameson laughed **up her sleeve** at this and told Bert he was talking **through his hat**. I had to **take my hat off to** her.

© Peter Collin Publishing, 1999
Based on the *English Dictionary for Students*, ISBN 1-901659-06-2

31

Confusing pairs and false friends

- <u>Confusing pairs</u> are two words which have a similar meaning to each other, but are used in a different way.
  or
  Are related to the same topic, but have a different meaning.
  or
  Look similar, but have a different meaning
- <u>False friends</u> are words in English which have a similar-looking word in another language but which have a different meaning.

Complete the following sentences with the appropriate word.

1. **actually / now**
    Please can we go home _____ ?
    It looks quite small, but _____ it is over 5 metres high.

2. **advice / advise**
    My grandfather gave me a very useful piece of _____ .
    I _____ you to put all your money into a deposit account.

3. **affect / effect**
    The cuts in spending will have a serious _____ on the hospital.
    The strike will seriously _____ the train service.

4. **already / yet**
    I haven't seen her _____ this morning.
    I've _____ done my shopping.

5. **afraid of / worried about**
    I am _____ snakes.
    She's _____ the baby; he doesn't look very well.

6. **avoid / prevent**
    The police will _____ anyone from leaving the building.
    You should travel early to _____ the traffic jams.

7. **beside / besides**
    Come and sit down _____ me.
    _____ managing the shop, he also teaches in the evening.

8. **bring / fetch**
    It's your turn to _____ the children from school.
    Don't forget to _____ the books to school with you.

9. **chance / possibility**
    Our team has a good _____ of winning tonight.
    There is always the _____ that the plane will be early.

10. **channel / canal**
    You can take a boat trip around the _____s of Amsterdam.
    Can you switch the television to _____ 4 for the news?
    England and France are separated by the _____ .

11. **conduct / direct**
    Von Karajan will _____ the Berlin Symphonic Orchestra at the concert.
    It took two policemen to _____ the traffic.

12. **continuous / continual**
    She has been in _____ pain for three days.
    I am getting fed up with her _____ complaints.

13. **driver / chauffeur**
    The _____ brought the Rolls Royce to the hotel's main entrance.
    He's got a job as a bus _____ .

14. **formidable / wonderful**
    They had a _____ holiday by a lake in Sweden.
    The castle is surrounded by _____ walls and gates.

15. **fun / funny**
    I didn't have much _____ on my birthday.
    He made _____ faces and made the children laugh.

16. **go / play**
Shall we _____ jogging or swimming?
Neither. Let's _____ tennis.

17. **come along with / follow**
Would you like to _____ me to the cinema tonight?
Make sure the dog doesn't _____ me to the shops.

18. **harm / damage**
Don't _____ my sunglasses if you borrow them.
He didn't mean to _____ your little girl.

19. **invent / discover**
Did Alexander Fleming _____ penicillin?
When did she _____ the new computer terminal?

20. **job / work**
He goes to _____ every day on his bicycle.
She's got a _____ in the supermarket.

21. **kind / sympathetic**
You should always be _____ to little children.
I'm very _____ to her problems.

22. **lay / lie**
I'm very tired; I'll just go and _____ down for a few minutes.
My father is going to _____ a new carpet in the dining room.

23. **lend / borrow**
Can I _____ you car to go to the shops?
He asked me if I would _____ him £5 till Monday.

24. **nature / countryside**
We must try to protect _____ and the environment.
The English _____ is beautiful in spring.

25. **pass / take**
She had to _____ her driving test three times before she was able to _____.

26. **practice / practise**
You need more _____ before you're ready to enter the competition.
Don't forget to _____ throwing and catching.

27. **priceless / valueless**
Be very careful with that painting; it's _____ .
Her jewels were all imitations; they were quite _____ .

28. **principal / principle**
She refuses to eat meat on _____ .
The _____ wants to see you in her office.
The country's _____ products are paper and wood.
We talked about the _____s of nuclear physics.

29. **raise / rise**
Does the sun _____ in the east or the west?
The airline are going to _____ their fares again next year.

30. **recipe / receipt**
Goods cannot be exchanged unless a sale _____ is shown.
I gave her an Indian _____ book for her birthday.

31. **remember / remind**
Would you _____ me to finish early tonight?
Did you _____ to switch off the kitchen light?

32. **scenery / view**
I adore the beautiful _____ in the Lake District.
You can get a good _____ of the sea from the church tower.

33. **sensible / sensitive**
She's very _____ and is easily upset.
Staying indoors was a _____ thing to do in this terrible weather.

34. **take / bring**
Can you _____ this cheque to the bank for me please?
Can I _____ my girlfriend here for tea?

Cooking and Eating

1. VERBS
*Read the text in the box below and match the words in **bold** with their definitions underneath. Use your dictionary to check your answers.*

> I recently went on a cookery course. It was very tiring work. First of all I had to learn how to prepare food. The teacher showed us how to **marinade** meat before we cooked it, **baste** it while it was cooking and even how to **slice** it once it had been cooked. We were also shown how to **chop**, **grate** and **dice** vegetables. I had never realised before how many different ways there are of cooking food; I had to learn how to **fry, bake, roast, grill, barbecue. stir fry** and **steam** it!. The best part of the course was trying out the food we had cooked. Some of the students would **nibble** the food cautiously and (in the case of the drinks we had prepared), **sip** delicately before they would **swallow**. I, on the other hand, would **gobble** and **gulp** it, sometimes without even bothering to **chew** it properly first!

1. to make something soft (☞soft) with your teeth.
2. to swallow food or liquid quickly.
3. to make food into small pieces by rubbing it over a metal tool.
4. to cook over a pan of boiling water by allowing the hot mist from the water to pass through small holes in a container (☞container) with food in.
5. to cook food outdoors on a metal grill over wood or charcoal (☞charcoal)
6. to soak meat or fish in a mixture of wine and herbs, etc, before cooking it
7. to eat something by taking small bites (☞bite).
8. to make food or liquid pass down your throat (☞throat) from your mouth to the stomach (☞stomach).
9. to eat greedily (☞greedy).
10. to pour melted fat and juices over meat as it is cooking.
11. to cut something into thin pieces
12. to cook food in oil or fat in a shallow (☞shallow) pan.
13. to cook food using very strong heat directly above it.
14. to drink something by taking only a small amount of liquid at a time.
15. to cut food into small pieces with a knife.
16. to cook vegetables or meat quickly in hot oil. Chinese food is often cooked in this way
17. to cook in an oven (☞oven) without any extra liquid or fat. Bread and cakes are usually cooked this way.
18. to cut food into small cubes (☞cube)
19. to cook food (especially meat) over a fire or in an oven.

2. NOUNS
Complete the sentences with the words or expressions in the box below.

recipe	menu	fast food	takeaway	tip
health foods	bill	ingredients	vegetarian	vegan
diet	starter	main course	dessert	side plate

1. I had soup as a ...., followed by chicken and chips for the ...... , with a .... of green salad, and finally a delicious .... of strawberries and cream.
2. My friend Tim is a ....; he won't eat meat. His girlfriend won't eat any food that involves animals (including eggs and cheese). She's a ....
3. In the restaurant, I chose my food from the ...., and when I had finished, paid the .... and left the waiter a small ....
4. I'm on a .... because I'm trying to lose weight, so I suppose I should eat more ...., but I'm afraid I can't resist hamburgers, pizzas and other ....
5. I bought a really good .... book last week, but can't find some of the .... I need for the dishes.
6. Shall we have dinner at home or shall we eat out? I know, let's do a bit of both. I'll go to the Chinese .... and bring something back.

© Peter Collin Publishing, 1999
Based on the *English Dictionary for Students*, ISBN 1-901659-06-2

3. IDIOMS, COLLOQUIALISMS AND OTHER EXPRESSIONS

*The expressions in **bold**, which all use words connected with food, have been put into the wrong sentences below. Use your dictionary to help you rearrange them.*

1. The exam was so easy! It was **a butter-fingers**.
2. I don't like horror films; they're **bananas**.
3. I don't get paid very much in my new job. In fact, my boss pays me **sour grapes**.
4. Jane is really angry with her boyfriend. As far as she's concerned, he's not **warm as toast**.
5. I've just seen the boss and he looks really angry. I think there's **a different kettle of fish**.
6. She became very embarrassed (☞embarrassed) and her face turned **cool as a cucumber**.
7. Mr Lewis is a wonderful man. He's **as different as chalk and cheese**.
8. You're mad, crazy, completely **not my cup of tea**!
9. I'm always dropping things and breaking them. I'm such **a piece of cake.**
10. Although Joe and Brian are brothers, they're completely different. They're **the salt of the earth**.
11. The bank robbers **were packed together like sardines** when the police questioned them, and told them everything they knew about the robbery.
12. I'm not at all cold. In fact, I'm **the flavour of the month**.
13. Andy is always calm and relaxed. He never panics (☞panic). He's **as red as a beetroot**.
14. Steven didn't congratulate (☞congratulate) me when I got the job. It was probably **peanuts**.
15. It was so crowded on the train we **spilled the beans**.
16. I don't mind you borrowing my umbrella without asking, but to borrow my car? That's **trouble brewing**.

Crime and the law

1. VERBS
Complete the sentences below with a word or expression from the box.

falsified smuggled sentenced burgled tried convicted arrested mugged break vandalized
stole robbed trafficking charged

Richard Mann has been committing crimes (☞crime / criminal) since he was a boy.

1. When he was only 15 he _____ telephone boxes and public toilets.
2. As he grew older, he _____ old ladies in the street and stole their money.
3. In his early twenties, he _____ private houses.
4. He also _____ banks, post offices and jewellery shops.
5. On one occasion, he _____ almost £20,000 from a post office.
6. In his late twenties, he _____ cigarettes and alcohol from one country to another.
7. During his only legitimate (☞legitimate, def a) job in an office, he _____ the accounts and pocketed (☞pocket, def 2) thousands of pounds.
8. He then started _____ drugs.
9. The police finally _____ him last year.
10. They _____ him with almost thirty crimes.
11. He was _____ at a Crown Court. (☞Crown Court).
12. He was _____ of all his crimes.
13. He was _____ to 15 years in prison.
14. He won't _____ the law again for a long time.

2. NOUNS
<u>Criminals and their crimes.</u> *Use your dictionary to look up the names of the crimes committed by the following criminals. You will usually find the answer directly above or below the main dictionary entry. The first one has been done as an example.*

Criminal	Crime
a burglar	burglary
a robber	
a shoplifter	
a vandal	
a rapist	
a hooligan	
a murderer	
a hijacker	
a forger	
a spy	
a pirate	
a terrorist	

© Peter Collin Publishing, 1999
Based on the *English Dictionary for Students*, ISBN 1-901659-06-2

3. NOUNS, VERBS AND ADJECTIVES

The law. _Use your dictionary to find the differences between the following sets of words._

1. _a judge_ and _a jury_
2. _a prison_ and _a remand centre_
3. _a solicitor_ and _a barrister_
4. _a witness_ and _a defendant_
5. _to arrest_ and _to charge_

5. _to acquit_ and _to sentence_
6. _corporal punishment_ and _capital punishment_
7. _innocent_ and _guilty_

4. IDIOMS, COLLOQUIALISMS AND OTHER EXPRESSIONS

Complete the following story using a word or expression from the box.

behind bars   nick   boys in blue   doing time   got away with   nicking
spill the beans   hardened   cops   as thick as thieves   leg it   red handed

Brian and Bert had always been 1._____, sharing each other's secrets and doing everything together. They turned to a life of crime in their teens, and by the time they were in their early twenties, they were already 2._____ criminals. They burgled houses and stole cars and always 3._____ it, discovering that they actually enjoyed the excitement of avoiding the 4._____. However, their luck didn't last and one day the 5._____ caught them 6._____ while they were 7._____ a car. They tried to 8._____, but didn't get too far. The police interviewed them and told them to 9._____. I'm glad to say that Ronnie and Reggie are now 10._____ in Wandsworth 11._____, and expect to be 12._____ for at least two years.

Describing people

1. CHARACTER AND PERSONALITY

Match the sentences in the left hand column with those in the right hand column. Use the adjectives in bold to help you.

1.	I wish John wouldn't be so **critical** all the time.	A. I know! He spoke non-stop for two hours on the telephone last night!
2.	Mary is so **witty**.	B. She made some really nasty remarks about the new secretary.
3.	Chris is such a **garrulous** person.	C. He hates it when I go out with my friends.
4.	Sometimes Rick can be really **impulsive**.	D. You can never make her change her mind.
5.	Laurence is the most **conceited** person I know.	E. You always believe that only bad things will happen.
6.	Mr Kelly is very **absent-minded**.	F. He loves going to parties.
7.	Jan is so **obstinate**.	G. After all, nobody's perfect.
8.	Mr. Roberts is extremely **reserved**.	H. It's very easy to upset her.
9.	You're not very **punctual**, are you?	I. You're almost never on time.
10.	Has anyone ever told you how **bossy** you are?	J. She always makes good decisions and does the right thing.
11.	You're so **pessimistic**!	K. That's true. She made a very clever and funny speech at her party.
12.	Jenny is **optimistic** about the future.	L. Her strong and unreasonable ideas have really upset some people.
13.	Brian is usually quite **reliable**.	M. She's always willing to listen to other people's ideas.
14.	Claire is very **sensitive**.	N. He often rushes to do things without thinking of the consequences.
15.	June is the most **sensible** student in the class.	O. Yesterday he went to the library in his slippers!
16.	My boyfriend is so **possessive**.	P. He thinks too much of himself.
17.	My mother is quite **open-minded**.	Q. I trust him completely.
18.	Jean should try not to be so **bigoted.**	R. She feels that everything will work out for the best.
19.	At times, Fiona can be really **bitchy**.	S. You're always telling people what to do.
20.	Mark is extremely **sociable**.	T. He never reveals his thoughts or feelings.

2. IDIOMS, COLLOQUIALISMS AND OTHER EXPRESSIONS

Look at the following list of words and expressions, and decide whether they are positive or negative. Use your dictionary to check the meanings.

1. a fuddy-duddy
2. a pain in the neck
3. a gossip
4. a troublemaker
5. a slob
6. a layabout
7. a wet blanket
8. a couch potato

9. a brick
10. a golden boy
11. a high-flyer
12. a windbag
13. a busybody
14. the salt of the earth
15. a slave driver
16. an early bird

17. a sponger
18. a bimbo
19. a jerk
20. a moron
21. a stick-in-the-mud
22. the life and soul of the party

© Peter Collin Publishing, 1999
Based on the *English Dictionary for Students*, ISBN 1-901659-06-2

Education

1. VERBS

Look at the sentences below and fill in the gaps using the appropriate word or expression from A, B or C.

1. He got a good grade in his maths, but _____ his English exam.
   A. passed   B. took   C. failed

2. She had to _____ her First Certificate exam three times.
   A. study   B. take   C. make

3. She _____ her driving test first time!
   A. passed   B. succeeded   C. won

4. He is _____ medicine because he wants to become a doctor.
   A. studying   B. learning   C. acquiring

5. He's _____ to speak French at college.
   A. studying   B. learning   C. teaching

6. She's _____ herself to speak Japanese.
   A. learning   B. studying   C. teaching

7. She _____ from Edinburgh University last year.
   A. left   B. graduated   C. passed

8. We need to _____ young people about the dangers of alcohol.
   A. educate   B. bring up   C. raise

9. I'm _____ for my history test tomorrow.
   A. learning   B. revising   C. remembering

10. School _____ next week; I can't wait for the holidays to begin!
    A. breaks into   B. breaks up   C. breaks down

2. NOUNS

A. *Look at the definitions below, and write the words they define in the grid on the next page. The first letter of each word has been given to you. If you do it correctly, you will find the name we give to a student at university in the shaded vertical strip. Use your dictionary to help you.*

1. A child at school.
   (eg, *The piano teacher thinks she is her best p _ _ _ _*)

2. A person who is studying at a college or university.
   (eg, *She's a brilliant s _ _ _ _ _ _*)

3. A diploma from a university.
   (eg, *She has a d _ _ _ _ _ in mathematics from Oxford University*)

4. A meeting of a small group of university students to discuss a subject with a teacher.
   (eg *The French s _ _ _ _ _ _ is being held in the conference room*)

5. A talk given to a class of students, usually at a university or college
   (eg, *We are going to a l _ _ _ _ _ _ on pollution*).

6. A sum of money to help
   (eg, *Not many students get a full g _ _ _ _*)

7. A teaching session between a tutor and one or more students.
   (eg, *We had a t _ _ _ _ _ _ _ on Russian history*)

8. All the people who work in a company, school, college or other organization
   (eg, *Three members of s _ _ _ _ are away sick*)

9. A person with a degree from a university.
   (eg, *He's a g _ _ _ _ _ _ _ of London University*)

10. An area of knowledge (☞knowledge , def a) that you are studying.
    (eg, *Maths is his weakest s _ _ _ _ _ _*)

11. The points given to a student for a test or a piece of work.
    (eg, *She got top m _ _ _ _ in English*)

12. A school that is funded
    (☞fund, def 2) by the state. (eg, *He went to a s_ _ _ _ _ _ _ _ _ _*)

13. A school for little children.
    (eg, *We send our youngest son to the local k_ _ _ _ _ _ _ _ _ _ _*)

1.						p							
2.	s												
3.					d								
4.					s								
5.	l												
6.					g								
7.		t											
8.				s									
9.		g											
10.				s									
11.				m									
12.		s											
13.		k											

B. *What's the difference? use your dictionary to help you find the difference between the following pairs of words.*

1. a <u>teacher</u> and a <u>professor</u>

2. a <u>primary school</u> and a <u>secondary school</u>.

3. a <u>fee</u> and a <u>grant</u>

4. a <u>term</u> and a <u>semester</u>

5. a <u>graduate</u> *in Britain* and a <u>graduate</u> *in the USA*.

6. a <u>state</u> school and a <u>public</u> school

3. IDIOMS, COLLOQUIALISMS AND OTHER EXPRESSIONS

Look at these sentences and decide which of the idioms and colloquialisms in **bold** *is correct. In each sentence, there are two expressions which we do <u>not</u> use in English.*

1. He gets up early to go to college, and comes home late. I keep telling him he shouldn't **buy a dog with two tails / burn the candle at both ends / try to wear two pairs of trousers.**

2. Sally always does her homework on time and buys the teacher little presents. The other children hate her. She's such a **teacher's toy / teacher's jewel / teacher's pet**.

3. He'll have to **pull his socks up / polish his head / empty his washing basket** and work harder or he'll fail his exams.

4. She didn't work hard enough and **flunked / splodged / squidged** her exams.

5. They didn't go to school, but **chased the tiger / emptied their heads / played truant** and went fishing instead.

© Peter Collin Publishing, 1999
Based on the *English Dictionary for Students*, ISBN 1-901659-06-2

Expressions with *Get*

1. DEFINITIONS

*Look at the expressions in **bold** in box A and choose a suitable definition for that expression in box B.*

A.

1.	I think Ben **got out of bed on the wrong side** this morning.
2.	We're planning a little **get-together** of people from the office.
3.	The manager began the meeting with a few comments and then **got down to brass tacks**.
4.	Jan and Richard **get on like a house on fire**.
5.	Rory and Jeannie are getting married? **Get away with you!**
6.	You'll **get the sack** if you talk to the boss like that.
7.	That humming noise is really **getting on my nerves**.
8.	He's **got a nerve** to ask for a day off.
9.	I rang the shops to try and find a new dishwasher, but **got nowhere**.
10.	When she asked him for money, he told her to **get lost**.
11.	OK everyone, we're a bit late so let's **get going**.
12.	**Got it!**
13.	Do you think he **got my meaning**?
14.	**Get a grip on yourself** - you've got an interview in half an hour.
15.	The president is having to **get to grips with** the failing economy.
16.	If they don't **get their act together**, they'll miss the last date for entries to the competition.
17.	How can I **get him off my back**?
18.	If I don't **get a rise** soon, I'll start looking for another job.
19.	I've **got out of the habit** of eating chocolates.
20.	Rainy weather always **gets me down**.

B.

A.	to be unsuccessful
B.	a meeting of friends
C.	to stop pestering (☞pester) someone
D.	to understand.
E.	to be dismissed (☞dismiss, def a) from a job.
F.	not to do something any more
G.	to start to deal with something
H.	Go away. Leave me alone.
I.	over-confidence or rudeness (☞rudeness)
J.	to start
K.	to receive an increase in salary
L.	to try to control yourself; to try to be less emotional (☞emotional)
M.	to start discussing the real problem
N.	Don't try to make me believe that.
O.	to start the day badly
P.	to make someone sad
Q.	to organise yourself properly
R.	to annoy (☞annoy) someone
S.	I've solved the problem
T.	to be very friendly with each other

© Peter Collin Publishing, 1999
Based on the *English Dictionary for Students*, ISBN 1-901659-06-2

2. COMPLETE THE SENTENCES

Complete these sentences with an expression from the previous section. You may need to change the verb form and the pronoun (eg, he, she) in some of the sentences.

1. We're best friends. We _____.

2. I don't have much money. I hope I _____ soon.

3. 12 across. 10 letters beginning with a 'd'. A book which lists words. Aha! _____! A dictionary, of course!

4. Our boss is in a terrible mood. I think he must have _____ .

5. I feel really unhappy in my job. It's really _____ .

6. _____! I don't believe you've won the lottery!

7. I'm studying Japanese and I'm just beginning to _____ the grammar.

8. I'm having a little _____ at my place tonight. Would you like to join us?

9. You want me to lend you my car after you crashed it the last time I leant it to you? You've _____!

10. I was so angry with him I told him to _____ .

11. We should _____ and talk about the real problems that are affecting the company.

12. Stop being so emotional. _____!

13. I told my boss I thought he was incompetent (☞incompetent, def a) . A few days later, I _____. I still haven't found another job.

14. You really should _____ of smoking so much - it's very bad for you.

15. He told me that my music really _____.

16. We're _____ with this problem. Let's take a break and come back to it later on.

17. She's always following me around and telling me what to do. I wish she would _____ .

18. The boss told me to _____ or I would lose my job.

29. I'm not sure they understood me. I hope they _____ .

20. If we don't _____ soon, we'll miss the train.

☞ *You will find more expressions using **get** in the* *phrasal verbs section on page 76.*

Health and fitness / The body

1. VERBS
Complete the text below with one of the words or expressions from the box.

fall ill   recuperate   examine   operate   take exercise   suffer   refer   treat   look after   keep fit
get well   cure   pick up

Most people believe it's very important to **1.**_____ in order to **2.**_____, but even the fittest person can sometimes **3.**_____, no matter how hard they **4.**_____ their health. If you do become ill, of course you want to **5.**_____ as soon as possible. With most minor illnesses, such as a cold or flu (☞flu), it's usually possible to **6.**_____ yourself by taking lots of rest and drinking plenty of liquid. However, if you **7.**_____ from something more serious, you will have to go to your doctor. He will **8.**_____ you and, if possible, **9.**_____ you with medicine which you can **10.**_____ from your local chemist. If you have an unusual illness, your doctor may **11.**_____ you to a specialist (☞specialist, def 1b) or a hospital, who may decide to **12.**_____ on you if your illness is serious. You will then have to **13.**_____, and this can take a long time.

2. NOUNS
A. *Medical words.* There are 12 words hidden in the box. Look at the definitions on the left and find the words that match them in the box. The first letter of each word has been given to you.

1. room where a doctor or dentist sees and examines a patient. (s)
2. person who looks after sick people. (n)
3. order written by a doctor to a pharmacist asking for a drug to be prepared and sold to a patient. (p)
4. doctor who specializes in surgery. (s)
5. department in a hospital for accident victims. (c)
6. sick person who is in hospital or who is being treated by a doctor, dentist, etc. (p)
7. room or set of rooms in a hospital, with beds for 6. above. (w)
8. person who studies and treats mental disease. (p)
9. agreed time for a meeting to see your doctor or dentist. (a)
10. medical specialist attached to a hospital . (c)
11. professional nurse who helps a woman give birth, often at home. (m)
12. change in the way a body works or looks, showing that a disease is present and has been noticed by the patient or doctor. (s)

p	p	r	e	s	c	r	i	p	t	i	o	n
s	c	a	s	u	a	l	t	y	c	k	a	p
s	p	s	m	r	s	c	a	n	p	y	p	w
c	w	w	p	g	e	g	b	d	f	j	p	s
p	a	t	i	e	n	t	w	z	y	p	o	y
a	r	b	c	r	u	d	e	f	g	t	i	m
r	d	q	p	y	r	o	n	m	l	b	n	p
s	t	c	o	n	s	u	l	t	a	n	t	t
q	s	u	r	g	e	o	n	m	m	s	m	o
i	o	i	y	r	m	i	d	w	i	f	e	m
y	j	h	g	f	d	s	a	z	x	c	n	s
p	s	y	c	h	i	a	t	r	i	s	t	x
w	o	p	i	u	y	t	r	f	d	s	a	c

B. _Parts of the body._ Look at the words on the next page and number them in order of height (for example, _forehead_ is at the top of the body, so is number 1; _Sole_ is at the bottom of the body, so is number 19).

forehead		1	forehead
sole		2	
stomach		3	
chest		4	
toe		5	
ankle		6	
hip		7	
shoulder		8	
eyebrow		9	
Adam's apple		10	
lip		11	
nostril		12	
knee		13	
thigh		14	
waist		15	
cheek		16	
throat		17	
groin		18	
shin		19	sole

3. IDIOMS, COLLOQUIALISMS AND OTHER EXPRESSIONS

A. _Feeling well / feeling sick._ How would you feel in the following situations?

1. You are **under the weather.** ☺ ☹
2. Your condition is **touch-and-go.** ☺ ☹
3. You look **washed out**. ☺ ☹
4. You have **come down with something.** ☺ ☹
5. You are **as fit as a fiddle**. ☺ ☹

6. You are **in good shape**. ☺ ☹
7. You have **taken a turn for the worse**. ☺ ☹
8. You are **not feeling yourself**. ☺ ☹
9. You are **laid up with something**. ☺ ☹

B. _Parts of the body._ Complete the sentences below using a word from the box.

nose   leg   neck   elbow   ear   foot   eye   hand   thumb   shoulder

1. He gave me a _____ with the washing up.
2. They had been going out together for some time, and then she suddenly gave him the _____ .
3. Don't worry. I wasn't being serious. I was only pulling your _____ .
4. I hoped she would give me a friendly welcome, but in fact she gave me the cold _____ .
5. Poor old Peter is dominated by his wife! She's got him under her _____ .
6. Can you keep an _____ out for the traffic warden while I go into the bank?
7. He's always annoying me! He's such a pain in the _____ .
8. He really put his _____ in it when he said his boss's wife was too fat: she was standing right behind him!
9. She thinks she's better than other people and always looks down her _____ at them.
10. Make sure you follow what is happening. Keep your _____ to the ground.

© Peter Collin Publishing, 1999
Based on the _English Dictionary for Students_, ISBN 1-901659-06-2

Human actions

1. GENERAL ACTIONS

Complete each of the sentences below with the most suitable word from the box. In some cases, more than one answer is possible.

fainted	shivered	fidgeted	sweated	trembled	nodded	dived	started	squatted	crouched
	dozed	stretched	leaned / leant	dragged	blushed				

1. He woke up, stood up and _____ his arms and legs.

2. The suitcase was too heavy to pick up, so she _____ it across the platform.

3. We _____ down to get through the low hole in the wall.

4. She _____ on the floor, trying to get the stains out of the carpet.

5. He _____ in and swam across the pool under water.

6. He _____ out of the car window and was almost hit by another car coming in the opposite direction.

7. She _____ in fear when she saw the lion come towards her.

8. She _____ with cold in the bitter wind.

9. The tennis players _____ in the hot sun.

10. She _____ with embarrassment when he spoke to her.

11. She _____ in surprise when she heard the loud bang.

12. She _____ when she saw the blood, and remained unconscious for about ten minutes.

13. She _____ off for a while after lunch and was suddenly woken up by the telephone ringing.

14. When he asked her if she understood the question, she _____ yes.

15. After an hour, he couldn't sit still any longer and _____ in his seat.

2. WAYS OF MOVING

Match the verbs on the left with the person who might behave in that way on the right.

Verbs	Person
hop	A. A man who has been injured in an accident but is still able to walk to the hospital.
dash	B. People walking in the park on a warm summer evening
crawl	C. A girl jumping across a wide stream of water
creep	D. Soldiers on parade
tiptoe	E. Someone who has hurt their foot and must move around on one leg.
leap	F. A young man running home to watch the football on television.
dawdle	G. Young children running, hopping and jumping along the road.
stagger	H. A very young baby who can't walk yet.
skip	I. A teenage daughter arriving home late and walking quietly up the stairs.
march	J. A boy walking quietly past a sleeping dog
stroll	K. A child walking very slowly to school

Based on the *English Dictionary for Students*, ISBN 1-901659-06-2

3. HAND AND ARM ACTIONS
Choose the correct verb in each of the following sentences.

1. He **punched / snapped / grabbed** me on the nose.

2. They all **punched / slapped / shook** him on the back to congratulate him.

3. The nurse **pointed / beckoned to / saluted** her to come into the room.

4. She **rubbed / wiped / stroked** the cat as it sat in her lap.

5. He **patted / wiped / folded** his pocket to make sure his wallet was still there.

6. He **snapped / grabbed / flexed** his suitcase and ran to the train.

7. It was dark in the cellar and he had to **grope / scratch / grab** for a light switch.

8. Ordinary soldiers must **salute / shake / point** their officers.

9. They **waved / punched / beckoned** goodbye as the boat left the harbour.

10. He **groped / scratched / stroked** his head as he wondered what to do.

11. He sat down and **tapped / crossed / folded** his arms.

12. Here's a handkerchief - **wipe / pat / rub** your nose.

13. You should always **pat / grope / shake** the bottle before you open it.

14. A policeman **tapped / scratched / stroked** him on the shoulder and arrested him.

15. He **shook / rubbed / wiped** his hands together to get them warm.

4. IDIOMS, COLLOQUIALISMS AND OTHER EXPRESSIONS
Look at the expressions in bold in the following sentences and decide if the definitions which accompany them are TRUE or FALSE.

1. She **made a beeline** for the chocolate cakes.
    She walked slowly towards the chocolate cakes.

2. **Once bitten, twice shy**.
    Once you have had a bad experience, you will not want to do it again.

3. The telephone's **on the blink**.
    The telephone is ringing.

4. We all gave Brian a **pat on the back**.
    We all congratulated Brian.

5. She **looked daggers** at me.
    She looked at me angrily.

6. He **ran like the wind**.
    He ran very fast.

7. We **salute** the firemen who entered the burning building to save lives.
    We are angry with the firemen.

8. **Don't look a gift horse in the mouth**.
    Don't be unkind to people who are less fortunate than you.

9. In the coffee break I went into the garden to **stretch my legs**.
    After sitting down for a long time, I went for a small walk.

10. Bob is not **fully stretched**.
    Bob is not very tall.

11. There was a **mad dash** to buy the tickets.
    Nobody wanted to buy the tickets.

12. Don't worry - I was only **pulling your leg**.
    I was only teasing (☞tease, def 1) you.

© Peter Collin Publishing, 1999
Based on the *English Dictionary for Students*, ISBN 1-901659-06-2

Love and relationships

1. A LOVE STORY: part 1

Complete the first part of the story below using the words and expressions in the box.

tie the knot	split up	engagement	got engaged	courting	living in sin
got on	wined and dined	attracted to	proposed	chatted her up	fallen in love
	asked her out	drift apart	cohabiting	go out	

Laurence first met Carol at a party and was immediately 1._____ her. He 2._____ and at the end of the evening 3._____ to dinner at a nearby restaurant. She accepted his offer and the next evening he 4._____ her in style, with champagne and delicious, exotic foods. They 5._____ well with each other, decided to meet again and then started to 6._____ on a regular basis. Laurence's granny was delighted that he was 7._____ at last. It wasn't long before they realised that they had 8._____ with each other.

A few months later, they bought a flat and moved in together. Laurence's granny disapproved of them 9._____, but Laurence explained that 10._____ was quite normal these days.

One day, Laurence decided to ask Carol to marry him, so after a romantic meal, he got down on one knee and 11._____ to her. They 12._____ and the next day announced their 13._____ to their friends and family. Their parents were delighted that they had decided to 14._____. Laurence's friends weren't so sure, however, and all agreed that they would 15._____ and 16._____ long before the wedding.

2. A LOVE STORY: part 2

Read the second part of the story and choose the correct word for each number.

A week or so before the wedding, Laurence went out on a **1.stag night / bull night / lion night** with his male friends, while Carol enjoyed her **2.chicken party / duck party / hen party** with her female friends.

At last, the big day arrived. Laurence and Carol had wanted to get married in a **3. registered office / registry office / regimental office**, but their parents insisted on a traditional church wedding. The church was packed, friends and family of the **4. bride / bright / blight** on the left, friends and family of the **5. gloom / groom / doom** on the right. Laurence sat nervously at the front with his **6. beast man / bent man / best man**, who was carrying the **7. wedding rings / wedding rinks / wedding rims** in his pocket. The organist started playing the **8. Wedding March / Wedding Crawl / Wedding Stagger** and Carol walked up the **9. aisle / I'll / ail**, accompanied by her father and followed by the **10. brightmaids / bridesmaids / bride's mates**. The priest conducted the ceremony and, after Laurence and Carol had exchanged **11. cows / vows / vowels**, pronounced them husband and wife.

The **12. wedding deception / wedding conception / wedding reception** was held at a local hotel. Laurence, the best man and Carol's father made speeches, and then everyone drank a **13. toast / toad / taste** to the happy couple. Later that evening, Laurence and Carol left for their **14. moneymoon / honeymoon / funnymoon**.

© Peter Collin Publishing, 1999
Based on the *English Dictionary for Students*, ISBN 1-901659-06-2

Topics

3. IDIOMS, COLLOQUIALISMS AND OTHER EXPRESSIONS

Match the sentences on the left with a suitable response on the right. Use your dictionary to look up the meanings of the words and expressions in bold.

1. They were going to get married, but at the last moment Allison **broke it off**.

2. I've got lots of friends, but only one real **soul mate**.

3. How do you get on with your **in-laws**?

4. Didn't you meet your future wife on a **blind date**?

5. I'm sorry you and Melanie have split up, but don't worry; there are **plenty more fish in the sea**.

6. Don't go out with him; he's a real **ladykiller**!

7. Sally came to the party with her latest **toy boy**.

8. Your new secretary is a bit of a **flirt**, isn't she?

9. Is Meg still **on the shelf**?

10. Chris and Jo's marriage is **on the rocks**.

11. How do you get on with your **ex- boyfriend**?

12. Are you **divorced**?

A. Me too. We have similar feelings and get on really well.

B. She certainly is. She likes attracting the attention of all the men in the office.

C. Not yet, but we are separated.

D. Yes. My friends arranged it for me.

E. That's true; I should get out a bit and meet more people.

F. Although we don't go out together any more, we're still good friends.

G. Poor Ian! He must have been really upset.

H. Really? I thought they were getting on so well together.

I. I know. He seems to spend all his time chatting up women.

J. Not well, I'm afraid. They've never forgiven me for marrying their son.

K. No. Haven't you heard? She met the man of her dreams a few weeks ago.

L. I'm not surprised. She's always preferred younger men.

© Peter Collin Publishing, 1999
Based on the *English Dictionary for Students*, ISBN 1-901659-06-2

Make or do?

1. WORDS USED WITH MAKE OR DO

Look at the sentences below and decide whether they should be completed with the verb <u>make</u> or the verb <u>do</u>.
*The form of these verbs will need to change in most sentences. Use the words in **bold** to help you.*

1. Has your mother _____ a **will** yet?

2. She _____ her piano **exercises** every morning.

3. The storm _____ a lot of **damage** last night.

4. Who will be _____ the **speech** at her wedding?

5. We _____ a large **profit** when we sold our house.

6. There's a lot of **work** still to be _____ .

7. At the moment he's _____ great **efforts** to learn Spanish.

8. They _____ a lot of **business** with European countries.

9. I'm not _____ the **washing** today.

10. When we got to the hotel, the **beds** hadn't been _____ .

11. The workmen are _____ so much **noise** we can't use the telephone.

12. We are _____ good **progress** towards finishing the house.

13. He didn't mean to _____ any **harm**.

14. His wife usually _____ all the **housework**.

15. The milk boiled over and _____ a **mess** on the stove.

16. I can't _____ today's **crossword** - it's too hard.

17. Are you going to _____ a Christmas **cake** again this year?

18. How much **money** did you _____ last year?

19. It took us hours to _____ the **washing up** after the party.

20. He _____ an **inquiry** about trains to Edinburgh.

21. I need to _____ a quick **phone call** before we leave.

22. Don't _____ such a **fuss** - it's only a little scratch.

23. She _____ a **mistake** in typing the address.

24. We _____ **friends** with some French people on holiday.

25. Our company is small but it's _____ **well**.

26. She _____ a few **notes** before her speech.

27. She was _____ the **ironing** when I came home.

28. Companies often _____ a **loss** in their first year of operations.

2. IDIOMS AND COLLOQUIALISMS USING *MAKE*

Replace the words and expressions in bold with an expression using make from the box.

make the best of   make a break with   made a meal of   make do with   make time   made off with
make-believe   make up my mind

1. The burglar **stole** all their silver.

2. She forgot her pyjamas and had to **use** a T-shirt **because there was nothing else available**.

3. They say it will rain this afternoon so we'd better **take advantage of** the sunshine while it's here.

4. I can't **decide** whether to take the afternoon off to do some shopping or stay in the office and work.

5. She **spent a lot of time and effort** repainting the kitchen **without really doing it well**.

6. His stories about his love affairs are just **not true, although he pretends they are**.

7. We must **arrange** to visit the new sports club **even though we are short of time**.

8. I've tried to forget my last girlfriend, but it's not always easy **to move away from** the past.

Based on the *English Dictionary for Students*, ISBN 1-901659-06-2

3. IDIOMS AND COLLOQUIALISMS USING *DO*

Complete the following sentences using a word which you will find hidden in the grid. One of the words is used twice. The first letter of each word has been given to you.

1. If the computer doesn't work, hit it - that should do the t_____.

2. Will you do the h_____ John and pour us all a drink?

3. He never uses violence himself, he just gets other people to do the d_____ work for him.

4. An evening out would do w_____ to cheer him up

5. She's very good at do-it-y_____ jobs.

6. If you live in the country, can you do w_____ a car

7. This chicken is done to a t_____

8. She told him all the do's and d_____ about working in the office.

9. He did me a good t_____, so I helped him in return

10. When we went to Barcelona, we did all the s_____ .

r	t	d	y	u	i	t	e	w	q	f	h
l	w	i	t	h	o	u	t	k	s	g	f
w	e	r	r	t	u	r	o	p	i	g	h
l	k	t	j	d	o	n	t	s	g	c	v
m	y	y	t	y	r	s	u	c	h	v	b
w	o	n	d	e	r	s	r	m	t	n	b
m	u	n	b	v	c	x	n	e	s	r	t
p	r	o	i	u	y	t	r	e	w	q	a
b	s	n	b	v	c	t	r	i	c	k	d
e	e	d	e	w	d	f	g	h	j	k	l
x	l	l	k	h	o	n	o	u	r	s	n
c	f	j	h	g	f	d	s	a	b	v	c

☞ *You will find more expressions using **make** and **do** in the <u>phrasal verbs</u> section on pages 75 and 78.*

© Peter Collin Publishing, 1999
Based on the *English Dictionary for Students*, ISBN 1-901659-06-2

Materials

1. ADJECTIVES AND NOUNS

*The words in **bold** are in the wrong sentences. Put them into the correct sentences. In several cases, more than one word is possible.*

1. He was wearing a pair of **timber** trousers.
2. We put the glasses into **polyester** boxes.
3. We used an old piece of **wool** as a roof for the hut.
4. She keeps her collection of precious Chinese **rubber** in a glass case.
5. After the rain, the dry **satin** on the football pitch suddenly turned wet and sticky underfoot.
6. He was wearing a pair of old **corrugated iron** shoes.
7. The house is surrounded by a high **silk** wall.
8. The carpet in our living room is made of **leather**.
9. Why are **cork** bedsheets so cold?
10. He was wearing a **porcelain** jacket.
11. She placed little **stained glass** mats on the table to stop the wine glass marking it.
12. He bought two **plastic** shirts in the sale.
13. She was wearing a beautiful **cardboard** scarf.
14. Canterbury Cathedral is famous for its **corduroy** windows.
15. She was wearing a thick **stainless steel** coat.
16. We take **fur** plates when we go for picnics on the beach.
17. She wore little red **iron** slippers.
18. She bought a white **wooden** tablecloth.
19. He was wearing a pair of blue **turf** shoes.
20. I bought her a set of **cotton** saucepans.
21. The roof is made with **denim** from an old ship.
22. I wore a pair of **suede** overalls when I painted the living room.
23. Car tyres are made of **canvas**.
24. There's an old **linen** table in the kitchen.
25. The old gates are made of **nylon**.
26. My new shoes have got **brick** soles.

2. GUESS THE OBJECT

Look at the following descriptions and decide what is being described in each one. You might find it useful to look at the unit on shape and size on page 61 to help you with some of the descriptions.

1. It's rectangular and made of plastic. It's flat. It measures about 8cm x 5cm. It can be a variety of colours. You can carry it in your wallet or purse.

2. It's round, with an open top and a flat bottom. It comes in different sizes. It's made of stainless steel or iron so it can stand a lot of heat.

3. Traditionally its triangular and made of canvas, although most modern ones are made of nylon and come in a variety of shapes and sizes.

4. It's cylindrical and made of light bark, although nowadays you can also find plastic ones. It's not very big. When you remove it, it makes a loud 'pop!'

5. It's made of plastic and iron. It's wide at one end and narrow at the other, with a plastic handle on top. Most of them are designed to spray water. The bottom part gets very hot.

8. It's an irregular shape, and it's made of china or porcelain. It has a handle, a spout for pouring and a lid. You should be careful not to drop it, as it will probably break if you do.

6. It's long, thin and made of fabric such as silk or cotton. It can come in a variety of colours and patterns. Men use them more than women, especially at work.

9. It's usually made of wool and is long, flat and rectangular. Football fans often have one with the name of their favourite team on. It's particularly useful in winter.

7. They're made of denim and are usually blue, although you often see them in black or white. They're very popular with younger people because they're casual and comfortable.

10. It's spherical and made of leather, although cheaper ones are made of plastic or rubber. It's about 30cm in diameter. It's usually white, even though it gets dirty quickly.

3. IDIOMS, COLLOQUIALISMS AND OTHER EXPRESSIONS

Look at the following sentences and choose the correct definition for the words and expressions in **bold**.

1.   Politicians try to be careful not to **wash their dirty linen in public**
   A. tell dreadful personal secrets about themselves and their family
   B. say bad things about other politicians
   C. drink, smoke or do other things that people might not like

2.   The estate agent tried to **pull the wool over our eyes**
   A. to charge us too much money
   B. to take our money with out giving them anything in return
   C. to deceive us by not telling us the true facts

3.   I don't have any cash with me. Do you take **plastic**?
   A. cheques
   B. credit cards and charge cards
   C. U.S. dollars

4.   We spent our last holiday **under canvas**
   A. In a beach resort
   B. In a very cheap hotel
   C. in a tent

5.   We **turfed out** our old office furniture
   A. sold
   B. threw out
   C. burnt

6.   The thief had a **cast-iron alibi**. (☞alibi)
   A. an alibi that cannot be disproved. (☞disprove)
   B. a very weak alibi
   C. a very unlikely alibi

7.   She will have to **steel** herself to say what happened
   A. she'll have to pretend to be sad
   B. she'll have to refuse to say what happened
   C. she'll have to get ready to do something that she does not like

8.   A lot of young people end up living in **cardboard city**
   A. a place where homeless people build themselves shelters out of pieces of cardboard
   B. their parents' home
   C. with their girlfriend or boyfriend

© Peter Collin Publishing, 1999
Based on the *English Dictionary for Students*, ISBN 1-901659-06-2

Money

1. VERBS
Look at the conversation between the bank manager and the customer, and fill in the gaps with an appropriate word from the box.

bank lend withdraw earn owe afford save deposit borrow spend pay back open

Manager: So, Mr Jensen. How can I help you?

Customer: I'd like to (1)_____ £5,000 to buy a new car and I was wondering if your bank could help me.

Manager: I see. Can I ask if you (2)_____ money to any other banks?

Customer: Yes; £800 to the MidWest bank.

Manager: Right. I need to ask you about your salary (☞salary). Could you tell me how much you (3)_____ each month, and how much of that you usually manage to (4)_____?

Customer: I make about £1,200 a month, and I usually (5)_____ most of that on rent (☞rent, def 1), bills, food and general living expenses. I usually have about £250 left at the end of the month.

Manager: If we agree to (6)_____ you the money, how much could you (7)_____ to (8)_____ each month?

Customer: About £200.

Manager: Well, that would probably be fine. Now, as you don't currently (9)_____ with us, you must (10)_____ an account (☞account, def 1a) here. We will then (11)_____ the £5,000 in that account, and as soon as it goes in, you can (12)_____ it.

2. NOUNS
Explain the difference between the following pairs or groups of words. Use your dictionary to help you.

1.   a <u>bank</u> and a <u>building society</u>

2.   a <u>current account</u> and a <u>savings account</u>

3.   a <u>withdrawal</u> and a <u>deposit</u>

4.   a <u>statement</u> and a <u>balance</u>

5.   <u>cash</u> and a <u>cheque</u>

6.   a <u>credit card</u>, a <u>debit card</u> and a <u>cheque guarantee card</u>.

7.   a <u>bill</u> and a <u>receipt</u>

8.   a <u>standing order</u> and a <u>direct debit</u>

9.   a <u>loan</u> and an <u>overdraft</u>

Now choose one word from each pair or group to complete the sentences below.

1.   The best place to invest (☞invest, def a) money, or borrow it when you want to buy a house, is a _____ .

2.   The advantage of a _____ is that you can take out money any time using a cheque book or cash card.

3.   My husband made a £500 _____ from the bank and then lost it!

4.   I have a _____ of £25 in my bank account.

5.   The _____ is made out (☞make out, def d) to Mr. Smith.

6.   I have a spending limit of £3,000 on my American Express _____ .

7.   Goods from this shop cannot be exchanged unless a sales _____ is shown.

8.   I pay my electricity bills by _____ . The electric company transfers (☞transfer, def 2a) the money from my bank account to theirs.

9.   I couldn't believe it when I looked at my bank statement. I had an _____ of nearly £500!

© Peter Collin Publishing, 1999

Based on the *English Dictionary for Students*, ISBN 1-901659-06-2

3. IDIOMS, COLLOQUIALISMS AND OTHER EXPRESSIONS

How would you feel, <u>happy</u> or <u>unhappy</u>, if you...

1. were <u>broke</u>?
2. were <u>hard up</u>?
3. were <u>well-off</u>?
4. were unable to <u>make ends meet</u>?
5. were able to <u>spend money like water</u>?
6. had just <u>paid through the nose</u> for something?
7. were <u>bankrupt</u>?
8. were <u>down on your luck</u>?
9. were <u>penniless</u>?
10. were <u>skint</u>?
11. were <u>loaded</u>?
12. were <u>in the black</u>?
13. were <u>in the red</u>?
14. were <u>on the dole</u>?
15. had <u>money to burn</u>?
16. had a lot of <u>dosh</u>?
17. were <u>strapped for cash</u>?

Put the expressions into the appropriate box below.

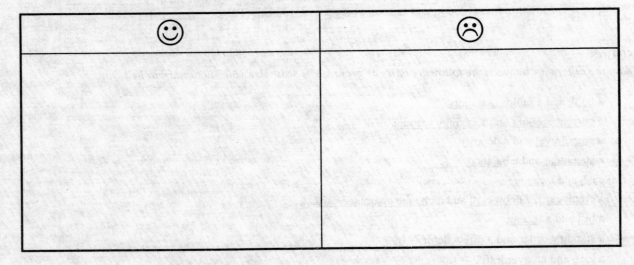

© Peter Collin Publishing, 1999
Based on the *English Dictionary for Students*, ISBN 1-901659-06-2

Nature and the environment

1. CLASSIFICATIONS

Put the words below into their appropriate box depending on their classification. (☞classification) . There are eight words for each box.

> cactus   fir   rose   salmon   bee   swan   seaweed   squid   owl   peacock   marigold
> ladybird   palm   human   lily   shark   parrot   squirrel   crab   seagull   bamboo   lobster
> tulip   orchid   trout   butterfly   crow   wasp   bat   snail   cedar   hedgehog   leopard
> daffodil   eagle   octopus   deer   dolphin   whale   oak   penguin   oyster   mushroom
> beetle   worm   ant   poppy   daisy

Mammals	Birds

Insects and invertebrates	Flowers

Trees and other plants	Sea and river creatures

Can you think of any other words to put into these boxes?

2. ANIMAL AND PLANT PARTS

*Look at this list of words and decide whether they are part of an animal (including birds and fish) or part of a plant. Circle **A** for animal or **P** for plant.*

> pollen (A / P)   wings (A / P)   leaf (A / P)   thorn (A / P)   beak (A / P)   bud (A / P)
> scales (A / P)   gills (A / P)   petal (A / P)   whiskers (A / P)   branch (A / P)   paws (A / P)
> twig (A / P)   trunk (A / P)   claws (A / P)   mane (A / P)   stalk (A / P)   hoof (A / P)   root (A / P)

Topics

3. THE ENVIRONMENT

Complete the following sentences with a word from the box.

CFC   endangered   tidal energy   ozone layer   desertification   fumes   greenhouse effect   pollution
acid rain   extinct   global warming   solar power   recycle   bottle bank

1. _____ falling on forests has killed a lot of trees in the last 20 years.

2. The council is encouraging us to _____ more household rubbish.

3. Factories and vehicles produce a lot of dangerous _____.

4. _____ of the atmosphere has increased over the last 50 years, making the environment very dirty.

5. The effect of gases in the earth's atmosphere is preventing the earth from losing heat; this is called the _____.

6. When _____ gases are released into the atmosphere, they rise slowly.

7. The hole in the _____ is getting larger every year.

8. If _____ continues, there is a danger that the polar (☞polar) ice-cap will start to melt.

9. We take all our empty bottles to the _____ for recycling.

10. Long periods of drought (☞drought) have brought about the _____ of whole areas of central Africa.

11. Tigers, whales and panda bears are all _____ species.

12. People are worried that soon whales will become _____.

13. We should use fewer fossil fuels (☞fossil fuels) and look to other energy sources such as _____ and _____.

4. IDIOMS, COLLOQUIALISMS AND OTHER EXPRESSIONS

In the grid on the right you will find the names of several animals. Use these to complete the sentences on the left. The first letter of each animal has been given to you after each sentence. (One animal is mentioned twice.)

1. A _____ in the hand is worth two in the bush. (b)

2. How do I know? A little _____ told me! (b)

3. He seems inoffensive, but actually he's a _____ in sheep's clothing (w)

4. He walked to school at a _____'s pace. (s)

5. She was so nervous before the exam she had _____ in her stomach. (b)

6. Don't count your _____ before they're hatched! (c)

7. I can't get her to agree; she's as stubborn as a _____ . (m)

8. The new airport is a complete white _____ (e)

9. Don't puzzle me; I hate it when you try to _____ me. (f)

10. Our company is having some serious financial problems. We're a lame _____ at the moment. (d)

11. It's been a long time since he came here. We haven't seen him for _____'s years!

12. It was a difficult problem, but he decided to take the _____ by the horns and tell his father he was leaving the family firm. (b)

w	g	y	u	i	f	r	m	d	g	w	h
a	d	h	e	r	o	b	u	l	l	d	w
w	o	t	l	s	x	d	l	g	d	r	x
w	n	k	e	n	k	u	e	w	o	l	f
a	k	c	p	a	m	c	l	r	g	b	y
k	e	c	h	i	c	k	e	n	s	i	t
f	y	f	a	l	x	e	q	j	l	r	f
b	v	c	n	x	z	w	b	i	r	d	k
b	u	t	t	e	r	f	l	i	e	s	e

© Peter Collin Publishing, 1999
Based on the *English Dictionary for Students*, ISBN 1-901659-06-2

Noises

1. HUMAN NOISES

Match the words in the box with their description below. Use your dictionary to check your answers.

sniff   sneeze   sigh   pant   scream   boo   gasp   stammer   cough   cheer   puff   chant
whisper   groan   yawn   snore

1. to sing a regular beat
2. to speak very quietly
3. to breathe with difficulty
4. to breathe fast
5. to make loud cries
6. to hesitate and repeat sounds when speaking
7. to make loud noises with the nose and throat when asleep
8. to send air out of your lungs suddenly because your throat hurts
9. to breathe deeply showing you are sad, relieved, etc.
10. to make a sound to show that you do not like an actor, politician, etc
11. to shout encouragement (☞encouragement)
12. to breathe in air through your nose
13. to open your mouth wide and breathe in and out deeply when you are tired or bored
14. to blow air suddenly out through your nose and mouth because of an irritation inside your nose (a reflex action)
15. to moan (☞moan, def 2a) deeply
16. to take a short, deep breath, showing surprise or pain.

2. ANIMAL NOISES

Match the noises on the left with the animals that make them on the right.

Noise	Animal
croak	bee
squeak	donkey
howl	wolf
quack	snake
buzz	cat
grunt	sheep / goat
hiss	duck
neigh	lion / tiger
bray	mouse
bleat	dog
crow	pig
roar	cock(erel)
bark	horse
miaow / purr	frog

Several of these noises can also be made by humans or other objects (eg, a powerful engine can <u>purr</u>). Use your dictionary to find out which ones.

© Peter Collin Publishing, 1999
Based on the *English Dictionary for Students*, ISBN 1-901659-06-2

3. OTHER NOISES

Match the noises in the box with the things that cause them.

> sizzle   rumble   boom   blare   murmur   ring   clink   whirr   rattle   bang   pop
> thud   tinkle   click

1.   a cork coming out of a bottle
2.   somebody falling over and hitting their head heavily on the floor.
3.   loud music or car horns.
4.   a very large gun, or an aircraft breaking the sound barrier
5.   bells
6.   windows in the wind or a baby's toy which is shaken
7.   a little bell which rings when you open a shop door
8.   two glasses touching each other
9.   a camera
10. sausages cooking
11. a train passing over a bridge or thunder in the distance
12. a group of people talking quietly
13. a door shutting suddenly
14. a small plane

4. COMPLETE THE SENTENCES

Most of the words in the tasks above can be either nouns or verbs. Use them to complete the following sentences. If the word is a verb, you will need to change its form.

1.   He _____ in surprise when he saw the bill.
2.   The crowds _____ anti-government slogans.
3.   His loud _____ *(plural)* kept her awake.
4.   The crowd _____ when the first marathon runners appeared.
5.   She rushed into the police station and _____ out 'he's - he's - he's after me, he's got - got - a knife'
6.   We heard a faint _____ from the corner of the field and found an injured lamb.
7.   The lion _____ and then attacked.
8.   The dog _____ every time he hears the postman.
9.   He _____ his fingers to get the waiter's attention.
10. He drives around with his radio _____ .
11. The wet logs (☞log, def 1a) _____ as we threw them on the fire
12. He was red in the face and _____ as he crossed the finishing line.
13. She gave a deep _____ of relief and put the phone down.
14. The cat rubbed against my leg with a loud _____

© Peter Collin Publishing, 1999
Based on the *English Dictionary for Students*, ISBN 1-901659-06-2

Opposites

- A lot of verbs and adjectives can be made into opposites by adding a prefix (eg, *agree* - *disagree*, *correct* - *incorrect*. 📖 Word forms page 13 - 21). However, in other cases, it is necessary to change some letters or use a completely different word in order to make an opposite.
  For example:
  cry = laugh   import = export   generous = mean   thick = thin

- Some verbs and adjectives can have more than one meaning, and so can have more than one opposite.
  For example: light
  The room is very *light* - - - The room is very *dark*
  This book is very *light* - - - This book is very *heavy*.

1. VERBS

Complete these sentences by using the opposite of the word in **bold**. *You will need to change the forms of some of the words. You will find the answers in the box.*

forbid / ban   receive   fail   hit   empty   forget   defend   deny   destroy   succeed   retreat   laugh
spend   win   depart / leave   lend   reject   fall   punish   loosen

1. She fell off the ladder and everyone _____ (**cry**)

2. Why do we _____ so much money on food? (**save**)

3. His business has _____ more than he expected (**fail**)

4. A lot of private property was _____ in the war (**create**)

5. What time does our coach _____ (**arrive**)

6. He _____ the bottle into the sink. (**filled**)

7. The car _____ the tree. (**miss**)

8. The simplest way to _____ them will be to make them pay for the damage they caused. (**reward**)

9. Don't _____ we're having lunch together tomorrow. (**remember**)

10. The exam was very difficult. Most of the students _____ . (**pass**)

11. We only _____ our tickets the day before we were due to leave. (**sent**)

12. I expect our team will _____ tomorrow. (**lose**)

13. He asked me if I would _____ him £5 till Monday. (**borrow**)

14. She flatly _____ his proposal of marriage. (**accept**)

15. She couldn't _____ herself against the attack. (**attack**)

16. The pound has _____ against the dollar. (**rise**)

17. He flatly _____ stealing the car. (**confess**)

18. Smoking has been _____ on trains. (**permit / allow**)

19. He _____ his shoelaces and relaxed. (**tighten**)

20. Napoleon _____ from Moscow in 1812. (**attack / advance**)

2. ADJECTIVES

*Replace the adjectives in **bold** with an opposite from the box. Some words in the box can be used more than once.*

tame	shallow	public	odd	artificial	mean	compulsory	lazy	tight	amateur	thick	live
strong	guilty	smooth	easy	sharp	dim	approximate	tough	present	permanent	stale
		light	high	minor	cool	soft	hollow			

1. **real** pearls
2. a **thin** slice of bread
3. an **energetic** student
4. a **bland** taste
5. a **professional** photographer
6. a **wild** animal
7. an **innocent** man
8. a **generous** person
9. a **serious** book
10. a **solid** log of wood
11. an **alcoholic** drink
12. an **intelligent** student
13. a **normal** person
14. an **easy** exam
15. **absent** students
16. a **weak** cup of coffee
17. a **heavy** meal
18. a **temporary** job
19. a **small** income
20. a **low** building
21. **fresh** air

22. **dead** animals
23. a **dim** light
24. a **deep** pool
25. a **rough** sea
26. **voluntary** military service
27. **exact** figures
28. a **private** affair
29. a **tender** steak
30. a **rough** wine
31. a **hard** chair
32. a **loud** voice
33. a **loose** pair of trousers
34. a **blunt** knife
35. **recorded** music
36. a **clever** manager
37. a **difficult** test
38. a **dark** blue shirt
39. a **fresh** loaf of bread
40. a **major** injury
41. a **frantic** nurse
42. a **warm** cellar

© Peter Collin Publishing, 1999
Based on the *English Dictionary for Students*, ISBN 1-901659-06-2

Shape and size

1. SHAPE.

A. *Match the words below with the picture that best represents each word.*

1. a pyramid   2. a cube   3. a crescent   4. a spiral   5. a cone
6. a rectangle   7. a triangle   8. a circle   9. a square   10. a cylinder   11. an oval

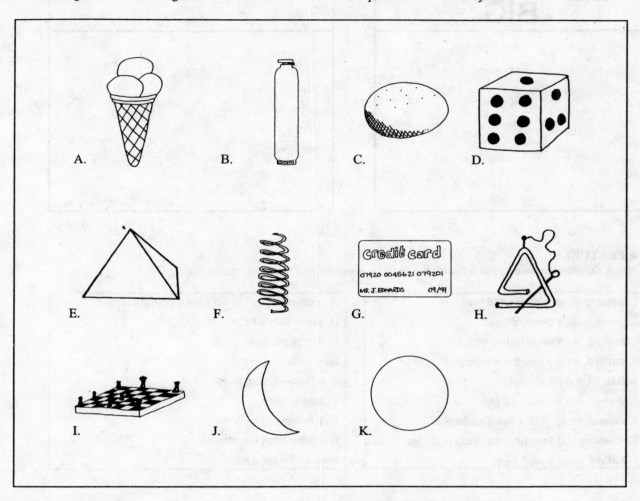

A.   B.   C.   D.

E.   F.   G.   H.

I.   J.   K.

B. *Look at the following list of words and decide what the correct adjective form is, A, B or C.*

1. sphere
   A. spherous   B. spherical   C. spherocous

2. cube
   A. cubed   B. cubous   C. cubal

3. cone
   A. conacular   B. conous   C. conical

4. rectangle
   A. rectanglous   B. rectanglis   C. rectangular

5. triangle
   A. triangular   B. trianglous   C. triangled

6. circle
   A. circled   B. circulous   C. circular

7. square
   A. square   B. squaret   C. squarous

8. cylinder
   A. cylindrous   B. cylindal   C. cylindrical

2. SIZE

Look at the following list of words and decide whether they can be used to describe something which is big or something which is small. Write each word in its appropriate box on the next page.

minute   enormous   minuscule   mammoth   huge   gigantic   tiny   monumental   colossal   massive giant   titchy   gargantuan   teeny (or teeny-weeny)

BIG	small

3. FEATURES

Match the descriptions on the left with the objects, geographical features, etc, on the right.

1. a **sharp** edge with **jagged** teeth.	A. a country road in very poor condition
2. **steep**, with a **pointed** peak.	B. somebody's hair
3. **rolling**, with **undulating** wheat.	C. a very old tree
4. **curved**, with a **smooth** surface.	D. a knife
5. **flat**, with **dotted** lines.	E. a slow-moving river
6. **wavy**, with blonde hi-lights.	F. a mountain
7. **meandering**, with a **calm** surface.	G. a banana
8. **winding** and **bumpy,** with deep potholes.	H. agricultural countryside
9. **hollow**, with **rough** bark.	I. an application form.

© Peter Collin Publishing, 1999
Based on the *English Dictionary for Students*, ISBN 1-901659-06-2

Shopping

1. VERBS
Look at the sentences below and fill in the gaps using the appropriate word or expression from A, B or C.

1.   What did you _____ your mother for her birthday?
     A. purchase   B. buy   C. acquire
2.   Why do we _____ so much money on food?
     A. spend   B. buy   C. sell
3.   I'll _____ you a pound to wash my car.
     A. spend   B. charge   C. pay
4.   Did you _____ the shoes in the shop before you bought them?
     A. put on   B. wear   C. try on
5.   Shop assistant: Can I help you?
     Customer: Yes please. I'm _____ the menswear (☞menswear) department.
     A. looking for   B. wanting   C. hunting for
6.   If the trousers are too small you can take them back and _____ them for a larger pair.
     A. sell back   B. exchange   C. replace
7.   (Angry customer to shop manager). I'd like to _____ about one of your members of staff.
     A. moan   B. groan   C. complain

2. NOUNS
A. *Where are they?* Look at the sentences on the left and decide where the speaker is. Choose from the list of shops on the right.

1. I'd like twelve red roses please.	
2. How much is that silver bracelet?	
3. I need a packet of envelopes and some writing paper please.	A. a record shop
	B. a department store
4. Do you have any photography magazines?	C. a florist's
	D. a stationer's
5. Is this cabinet (☞cabinet, def a) 17th or 18th century?	E. a chemist
	F. a jeweller's
6. Take the escalator (☞escalator) to get to menswear.	G. an antiques shop
	H. a newsagent's
7. Have you got anything for a sore throat?	
8. Do you have the latest album by Oasis?	

B. *Check your spelling.* One word in each of the following sentences is incorrectly spelt. Use your dictionary to help you correct them.

1.   I'd like my money back. I'd like a refound.
2.   £35 for a new television. What a bargein!
3.   It usually costs £150, but I got it for £75 in the sails.
4.   I don't like to buy things by male order - you never know exactly what you're going to get.
5.   Don't forget to get a reciept from the sales assistant in case you need to return it to the store.
6.   The lapel on the jacket says 'Wash in cold water only'.
7.   I'm afraid your cashear has overcharged (☞overcharge) me.

Topics

C. _Quantities_. _Complete the sentences below with the container or quantity that we usually buy the object in (for example, a **can** of Coke). Write the word in the grid on the right. If you do it correctly, you will find the name of another container in the shaded vertical strip._

A .... of biscuits
A .... of jam
A .... of chocolate
A .... of toothpaste
A .... of matches
A .... of soup

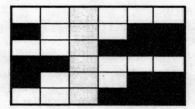

3. IDIOMS, COLLOQUIALISMS AND OTHER EXPRESSIONS

Look at the following sentences and decide whether the words and expressions in **bold** refer to a <u>small</u> amount of money or a <u>large</u> amount of money. Use your dictionary to help you.

1. The shoes in that shop cost **a fortune**.
2. That car was **a rip-off**!
3. He **paid through the nose** for his ticket to Hong Kong.
4. Our local petrol station sells **cut-price** petrol.
5. The repairs to his car cost him **an arm and a leg**.
6. She bought it **for a song** in a flea market. (☞flea market)

Now look at these sentences and decide if they are <u>true</u> or <u>false</u>:

1. If something is **selling like hot cakes**, not many people are buying it.
2. You spend a lot of money when you go **window shopping**.
3. It's a good idea to **shop around** for the best price before you buy something expensive.
4. If you buy clothes **off-the-peg**, you have them specially made for you.
5. If you **talk shop**, you discuss your favourite shop with a friend.
6. A **body shop** is a shop which arranges funerals (☞funeral, def a).

64

Sport

1. VERBS
Look at the sentences below and fill in the gaps using the appropriate word or expression from A, B or C.

1. Does Eddie _____ rugby for the university?
    A. do   B. make   C. play

2. You should _____ some exercise every day if you want to lose weight.
    A. take   B. make   C. play

3. They often _____ jogging (☞jog) in the streets near their home.
    A. make   B. go   C. do

4. I expect our team will _____ the game tomorrow.
    A. succeed   B. gain   C. win

5. I hope our team doesn't _____ the match on Saturday.
    A. lose   B. fail   C. defeat

6. Our football team will have to _____ France 2:0 if they want to get a place in the World Cup final.
    A. win   B. succeed   C. beat

7. If the two players _____, they will have to play the game again.
    A. equal   B. match   C. draw

8. You will need to _____ hard to get a place on the Olympic team.
    A. train   B. develop   c. learn

9. If our team manages to _____ another goal, they'll be national champions!
    A. hit   B. score   C. enter

10. Which football team do you _____ ?
    A. support   B. encourage   C. accept

2. NOUNS
A. *Venues and equipment*. Match the sports in the left-hand column with the venue (☞venue) in the centre column and an item which you associate with that sport in the right-hand column. There are two items which do not belong.

		trunks
swimming	range	gloves
tennis	racetrack	target
football	ring	strip
ice hockey	pool	helmet
horse-racing	racecourse	racket
shooting	court	bow
motor racing	rink	saddle
boxing	pitch	stick
		shuttlecock

B. _Jumbled words_. *Rearrange the letters in the box on the next page to find some more words related to sports. The first letter of each word is in **bold**. The clues after each jumbled word will help you.*

imudast:	a large building for sports, with seating arranged around a sports field.
eerrfee:	a person who supervises (☞supervise) a game, making sure that it is played according to the rules.
irepm**u**:	similar to the above, but usually associated with tennis or cricket.
senilanm:	an official who stays on the sideline (☞sideline, def 1b) in a ball game to see if the ball goes over the line.
attropesc:	a person who watches a football game, a horse show, etc.
ryelpa:	a person who plays a game
teehlta:	a sportsman who competes (☞compete) in races, etc.
raobdsocer:	a large board on which the score in a game is shown as the game progresses
porsupret:	a person who encourages a football team
naaer:	a building where sports, fights etc are held.

3. IDIOMS, COLLOQUIALISMS AND OTHER EXPRESSIONS

Look at the words and expressions below and decide which sports or games they are connected with. Use your dictionary to help you. Write the words in the grid on the right. If you do it correctly, you will reveal the name of a famous English football team in the shaded vertical strip.

1. Bulls eye!
2. pole position (2 words)
3. neck and neck (2 words)
4. On your marks ...get set...go!
5. Seconds out!
6. Foul!
7. Fore!

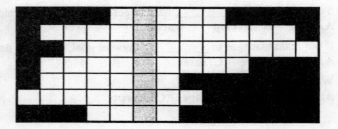

© Peter Collin Publishing, 1999

Based on the *English Dictionary for Students*, ISBN 1-901659-06-2

Travel and Holidays

1. VERBS.

A. *The sentences below describe the different stages (☞stage, def c) of a holiday. Unfortunately, they are in the wrong order. Rearrange them so that they are in the correct order. The first one has been done for you. Use your dictionary to help you find the meaning of the words in* **bold***.*

(   )   A few weeks later I went to the airport and **checked in** for my flight.

(*1*)   I **picked up** some holiday brochures (☞brochure) from the travel agency.

(   )   I spent the next two weeks **sunbathing** on the beach and **sightseeing** in the local area.

(   )   Three hours later, we **landed**.

(   )   I **picked** the holiday I wanted.

(   )   I left the airport and two hours later arrived at my hotel, where I **checked in**.

(   )   I found my seat and **fastened** my safety belt (☞safety belt).

(   )   The flight **took off** at 10 o'clock.

(   )   I then **booked** my holiday.

(   )   It was with a great deal of reluctance (☞reluctant) that I eventually **checked out** of the hotel and returned home.

(   )   All the passengers **disembarked**.

(   )   I did some shopping in the duty free (☞duty free) and then **boarded** my flight.

(   )   I **browsed** through the brochures.

B. *A lot of people like travelling, but a some dislike it. Look at the following sentences and decide how each person feels. Write their names in the box below.*

1. Bob adores it
2. Jo is keen on it
3. Bazil hates it
4. Jane loathes it
5. Mark is fond of it
6. Eric is mad about it
7. Penny can't stand it
8. Elsa gets bored with it
9. Vicky detests it

These people *like* travelling:	These people *dislike* travelling:

2. NOUNS

A. *Types of holiday. Look at the types of holiday on the left, and match them with the places you think you might stay in on the right. Most have more than one answer.*

Type of holiday	Places
1. a package holiday	
2. a camping holiday	A. a tent
3. a cruise	B. a hotel
4. a skiing holiday	C. a resort
5. a safari	D. a youth hostel
6. a walking holiday	E. a caravan
7. a sailing holiday	F. a guesthouse
8. a caravanning holiday	G. a boat's / ship's cabin
9. a sightseeing holiday	H. a villa / chalet

B. *Look at the sentences below, and fill in the gaps with an appropriate word from the box.*

tour operator shoulder bag passport travel agency tour foreign currency voyage excursion trip
journey insurance aisle boarding card (USA = boarding pass) traveller's cheques suitcase

1. We're planning a(n) _____ to the seaside at the weekend.

2. The _____ from Southampton to New York by ship took about five days.

3. The best way to see London is by taking a guided _____.

4. Last year they went on a train _____ across China.

5. James is going on a business _____ to Singapore next week.

6. We went to the _____ on the High Street to book our holiday, but they were informed by the _____ that there were no more places left.

7. (At the airport check-in desk) Would you like a seat by the window or one by the _____?

8. Here's your ticket and _____. You're in 33B. It's a no smoking seat.

9. I've just made a list of the things I need to take on holiday with me. First of all I need my _____ so that I can enter the country. I must get _____ in case I have an accident or lose something important. I have to go to the bank to get some _____ and _____. Oh, and of course I need my _____ to carry my clothes and other things. I'll also take a _____ so that I can carry my camera, some books and other bits and pieces.

3. IDIOMS, COLLOQUIALISMS AND OTHER EXPRESSIONS

Match the sentences on the left with a suitable reply on the right. Use your dictionary to check the meanings of the expressions in **bold**.

<u>HE SAID:</u>	<u>SHE REPLIED:</u>
1. Where shall we stay?	A. Really? I prefer to go somewhere a bit quieter, **off the beaten track**.
2. Can you recommend a good guest house in this area?	B. Wow! I didn't realise you were such a **globetrotter**!
3. Last year I went to Australia, Canada, Brazil, Argentina and China.	C. Poor you! You spent a whole day **on the road**.
4. How are we going to get home? We haven't got enough money for a taxi.	D. Let's **stop** at the first hotel we find.
5. Last year, we went to one of those resorts where everything - food and drink - is free.	E. I would hate to **live out of a suitcase** like that.
6. You don't have much luggage (☞luggage) with you.	F. Why don't we **thumb a lift**?
7. On my first visit to Indonesia, I found everything so different from England.	G. It sounds great. I've never been on an **all-inclusive holiday**.
8. We left London at 7 o'clock in the morning and didn't arrive in Inverness until 8 in the evening!	H. Yes, there's a nice B & B around the corner.
9. I love going to busy, lively resorts for my holiday.	I. I know. I prefer to **travel light**.
10. I spend most of my life travelling, moving from one hotel to the other.	J. I experienced similar **culture shock** when I went to Vietnam.

© Peter Collin Publishing, 1999
Based on the *English Dictionary for Students*, ISBN 1-901659-06-2

24 Hours

1. VERBS.
Look at the sentences below and fill in the gaps using the appropriate word or expression from A, B or C.

1. My alarm clock _____ at half past six..
    A. goes up   **B. goes out**   **C. goes off**

2. The first thing I do every morning is _____.
    A. get up   **B. wake up**   **C. sit up**

3. I have a shower and _____ my teeth.
    A. brush   **B. comb**   **C. sweep**

4. When I get dressed, the first thing I _____ is my shirt.
    A. put on   **B. wear**   **C. try on**

5. After breakfast, I _____ to the bus stop.
    A. speedy   **B. quickly**   **C. hurry**

6. After work, I _____ the children from school.
    A. pick up   **B. pick out**   **C. pick on**

7. Just before I go to bed, I _____ the cat _____.
    A. put...off   **B. put...out**   **C. put...up**

8. The last thing I do before I go to bed is _____ the alarm clock.
    A. prime   **B. set**   **C. prepare**

2. NOUNS
A. *Below you will see a list of things we use or wear at home or at work. Put them into the box where we use / wear them most often.*

shaver	briefcase	pyjamas	ring binder	nightie	iron	tumble drier	ironing board	kettle
computer	refrigerator	vacuum cleaner	fax	hair dryer	dishwasher	e-mail	filing cabinet	
hairbrush	microwave oven	suit	internet	slippers	file	dressing gown	business card	apron

Things we use / wear at home	Things we use / wear at work

B. <u>Complete the sentences</u>. *Now complete the sentences using one of the words above.*

1. You can contact me by phone or _____ if you want.

2. I never put the silver in the _____; it would ruin (☞ruin, def 2a) it.

3. I bought two pairs of _____ in the sale.

4. Each bathroom in the hotel is equipped with a _____ .

5. He put all the files (☞file, def 1b) into his _____ .

6. Post it to me, or send a _____ .

7. I've just put the _____ on so we can all have a cup of tea.

8. Put the dish in the _____ for three minutes, but make sure the food is piping hot
    (☞piping hot, def 2) before you eat it.

3. IDIOMS, COLLOQUIALISMS AND OTHER EXPRESSIONS

A. *Match the words and expressions in **bold** on the left with their definition on the right.*

1. Sarah staggered (☞stagger, def 1b) into work at ten o'clock, **bleary-eyed**.

2. I can't wait until Saturday comes. Then I can **have a lie-in**.

3. After his 12-mile walk, he **slept like a log**.

4. The doctor told him to **take things easy** after his operation.

5. His taxi was stuck in the **rush-hour** traffic.

6. Mary works the **night shift**.

7. She comes home every evening, **worn out** after a busy day at the office.

8. Jessie's a **night owl** and finds it difficult to get up in time for work.

9. We only go to the theatre **once in a blue moon**.

10. I had to get up at some **unearthly hour** to catch the plane to Milan.

11. If we want to miss the traffic, we must set off at the **crack of dawn**.

12. He's an **early bird**.

A. Much too early.

B. The time of day when traffic is bad, trains are full, etc.

C. Very tired.

D. To stay in bed longer than usual.

E. As soon as it starts to get light.

F. Someone who likes to work, eat, etc, until late at night and does not get up early in the morning.

G. Someone who likes to get up early and work before breakfast, and who does not stay up late at night.

H. Very rarely.

I. Sleep very soundly (☞soundly).

J. With eyes half closed from lack of sleep.

K. Work during the night.

L. To rest, not to do any hard work.

B. *The sentences below all use expressions with the word* time. *Unfortunately, the expressions are all in the wrong sentences. Rearrange them so that they are in the correct sentences.*

1. Don't hurry me. I like to **time after time**.

2. Bring back your boat; your **in time**.

3. **Pressed for time** I think he's quite mad.

4. They drove fast and got to the station just **for the time being** to catch the train.

5. She's never **at times** for meetings.

6. He's very old-fashioned; he's way **time's up**.

7. I've told her **waste time** not to do it, but she never listens to me.

8. Don't **take my time** putting your shoes on; just go and answer the door in your bare (☞bare, def 1a) feet.

9. We're in a hurry; we're a bit **behind the times**.

10. **On time** I'm staying at my mother's while I'm waiting for my flat to be redecorated.

© Peter Collin Publishing, 1999
Based on the *English Dictionary for Students*, ISBN 1-901659-06-2

The weather & natural phenomena

1. BAD WEATHER.

*Use the words in the box to complete the text below. Then use your dictionary to check the meanings of the nouns and adjectives in **bold**.*

mist frost sleet rain hail wind fog smog snow blizzard lightning thunder

Listen to the **pouring** (1)_____ outside, and the **roar** of the (2)_____ as it blows through the trees.
Listen to the **clatter** of icy (3)_____ on the window and the **crashing** of the (4)_____, while (5)_____
flashes across the sky. See the thick, grey (6)_____ and the thin, grey, wet (7)_____. Smell the
dirty, **bitter**, yellow-grey (8)_____ in the city. Feel the **crunch** of (9)_____ under your feet as you
walk on the icy grass, and shake the **freezing**, wet (10)_____ and (11)_____ from your hair as the
howling (12)_____ turns the world to white.

2. EXTREME WEATHER AND NATURAL PHENOMENA

*Look at the words below and decide which definition, A, B or C, best describes each one. Then check your
answers in your dictionary.*

1. **hurricane**
   (A) a storm over high mountains, usually accompanied by snow.
   (B) a tropical storm with strong winds and rain.
   (C) a very quick, but very heavy, rain shower.

2. **tornado**
   (A) a long, heavy snow shower, accompanied by strong winds.
   (B) a long period when there is no rain and when the land is dry.
   (C) a violent storm with a whirlwind (☞whirlwind, def a)

3. **volcano**
   (A) a violent shaking of the earth's surface.
   (B) a strong wind caused by a drop in air pressure (☞pressure, def b)
   (C) a mountain with a hole in the top through which lava (☞lava), ash and gas can come out.

4. **drought**
   (A) a storm, usually without rain, which happens in hot countries.
   (B) a very long period of rain.
   (C) a long period when there is no rain and when the land is dry.

5. **flood**
   (A) a large amount of water over land which is usually dry.
   (B) a large area of dry land which should usually be wet (eg, a dry lake).
   (C) a lake or river which has been poisoned (☞poisoned, def 2b) by pollution.

6. **earthquake**
   (A) a long, heavy snow shower, accompanied by strong winds.
   (B) a shaking of the earth caused by, for example, volcanic activity.
   (C) a large area of dry land which should usually be wet.

7. **tsunami**
   (A) a tropical storm with strong winds and rain.
   (B) a huge wave (☞wave, def 1a) in the sea, caused by an underwater earthquake.
   (C) a long period when there is no rain and when the land is dry.

3. WEATHER WORD FORMS

Complete the table below to show the verbs and adjectives which we use for the nouns in the left-hand column.

NOUN	VERB	ADJECTIVE
rain		
sun		
storm		
snow		
wind		

4. IDIOMS, COLLOQUIALISMS AND OTHER EXPRESSIONS

Replace the words and expressions in **bold** *with a suitable word or expression from the box.*

under a cloud	weather	bucketing down	boiling	steals my thunder	every cloud has a silver lining
on cloud nine	storm in a teacup	under the weather	cats and dogs	downpour	heavy weather of it

1.   It's raining **a lot.**

2.   It's **pouring with rain.**

3.   It's **very hot** in our office at the moment.

4.   We could ask him to sort out the invoices, but he'll make **it unnecessarily difficult and complicated.**

5.   Jan's feeling **unwell.**

6.   There was a sudden **heavy fall of rain** and all the spectators ran inside.

7.   I don't know if we can **survive** this crisis without any extra cash (☞cash, def 1).

8.   **However gloomy** (☞gloomy, def a) **things may seem, there is always some aspect which is good.**

9.   They were **very happy** when they won the lottery.

10. Ben was **under suspicion** (☞suspicion, def a) for a long time after the thefts were discovered.

11. Whenever I have a great idea, Penny **spoils it by doing it first and getting all the credit.**

12. Sarah thought it was important, but in fact it was a **lot of fuss** (☞fuss, def 1) **about something which was very trivial.**

Work

1. VERBS

*Read the text in the box below and match the words in **bold** with their definitions underneath. Use your dictionary to check your answers.*

> Brian James left University and decided to **apply for** a job which he saw advertised in the paper. He **filled in** the application forms and, a few weeks later, was asked to **attend an interview**. He was offered the job that same day.
>
> As he lived in a small town outside the city, he had to **commute** every day. He was good at his job and very soon was **promoted**. However, the company he worked for was having problems. Two people were **dismissed** for stealing and two of their friends **resigned** in sympathy (☞sympathy, def b), the directors decided to **lay off** five more because the company couldn't afford (☞afford) to keep them, and the managing director decided to **retire** early. The atmosphere was so bad that Brian eventually decided to **hand in his notice**.

1   to give up (☞give up, def a) a job.

2   to ask for a job, usually by writing a letter.

3   to be removed from a job, usually because you have done something bad.

4   same as 1.

5   to stop work and take a pension (☞pension, def 1), usually when you are in late middle age (☞middle age)

6   to write in the empty spaces on a form (☞form, def 1b)

7   to be given a better job in the organization you work for.

8   to be questioned by one or more people when you are applying for a job so that they can decide if you are suitable for that job.

9   to travel to work from home each day, usually from one town to another.

10   to be dismissed from your job for a time until more work is available.

2. NOUNS

Read the text which follows and fill in the gaps with an appropriate word from the box below. Use your dictionary to help you. In some cases, more than one answer is possible.

> commission prospects candidates references manager salary promotion applicants increment vacancy employee perks qualifications shortlist pension salesman

A computer company had a (1)_____ for position of (2)_____, and decided to advertise for a new (3)_____. A lot of (4)_____ with good (5)_____ and (6)_____ applied for the job, and after all the interviews had finished, the directors made a (7)_____ of the best (8)_____, then invited them to come back for another interview.

The person who eventually got the job was very happy. After all, he would receive an annual (9)_____ of £25,000, with a 5% (10)_____ twice a year, a 15% (11)_____ for each computer he managed to sell, excellent (12)_____ such as private health insurance and a company car, a company (13)_____ to make sure he would be well-off (☞ well-off) when he retired, and the chance of (14)_____ from salesman to sales (15)_____ if he was successful. All in all, his future (16)_____ looked very good.

© Peter Collin Publishing, 1999

Based on the *English Dictionary for Students*, ISBN 1-901659-06-2

Topics

3. IDIOMS, COLLOQUIALISMS AND OTHER EXPRESSIONS

*Match the sentences on the left with an appropriate sentence on the right. The sentences on the right include an idiom or colloquialism connected with work in **bold**. Use your dictionary to help you.*

(1) My brother is a manual (☞manual, def 1a) worker in a factory.

(2) My cousin is a secretary in an office.

(3) I need to do some more hours at work so that I can make more money.

(4) The train drivers are refusing to work.

(5) I work from 10.00pm to 6.00am.

(6) I work for a very small amount of money.

(7) Jo is unemployed (☞unemployed) and receiving unemployment benefit (☞benefit, def 1b).

(8) Jim applied to his boss for more money.

(9) Our boss makes his staff work too hard.

(10) Bob works too hard. Yesterday, he started at 7.30 in the morning and didn't finish until almost midnight!

(11) Our company director was given a large sum of money when he retired before the end of his contract (contract, def 1).

(12) Sarah has great potential and ambition.

(13) My boss made a mistake and made me take responsibility (☞responsibility) for it.

(14) Our company is still working in the usual way in spite of difficulties.

(15) Steve has an unusual job; he looks for top managers and offers them jobs in other companies.

(16) Have you heard? John has been dismissed for coming late all the time.

(A) She's always been a **high-flyer**.

(B) He **put in for a rise**.

(C) Like me, he's a **blue collar worker**.

(D) He's such a **slave driver**!

(E) I'm glad to say it's **business as usual.**

(F) Of course, I get paid more for working the **night shift**.

(G) If he continues like that, he'll **burn himself out.**

(H) I really hate working **for peanuts**.

(I) I think I'll ask if I can **work overtime**.

(J) They've decided to **come out on strike.**

(K) I hate it when I have to **carry the can** for someone else.

(L) I wish I could get a **golden handshake** like that!

(M) Like me, he's a **whitecollar worker**.

(N) I always knew he'd get **fired** one day.

(O) He's a **headhunter**.

(P) There's nothing worse than being **on the dole**.

<cue>74   © Peter Collin Publishing, 1999
Based on the *English Dictionary for Students*, ISBN 1-901659-06-2</cue>

Phrasal Verbs *Come*

Match the sentences in the left-hand column with those in the right-hand column. Use the phrasal verbs in bold to help you.

1. We **came across** this little restaurant when we were out walking.	A. Oh dear. It's such an unpleasant disease.
2. The children have **come down with** measles (☞measles).	B. He was obviously a bit nervous as the officer got closer
3. The policewoman **came up to** him and asked to see his passport.	C. I'm not surprised. I knew they'd get in the way.
4. Jenny **came into** a fortune when she was twenty-one.	D. Really? Where did you find it?
5. Simon's **come out in** a rash (☞ rash, def 1).	E. He's always saying something unexpected.
6. When we suggested moving to another office, we **came up against** a lot of opposition from the management.	F. For how long had she been unconscious (☞unconscious, def 1)?
7. The message **came through** this morning.	G. How could it? The phone has been disconnected (☞disconnect) and the fax machine is broken.
8. **Come along**, or you'll miss the bus.	H. You're always in such a hurry. Let me take my time.
9. Our team **came off** badly in the competition..	I. I'm not surprised. I didn't think they'd do very well.
10. When she **came to**, she was in hospital.	J. My son has developed one as well on his chest.
11. Richard **came out with** a really strange idea the other day.	K. Lucky her! Who did she inherit (☞inherit, def a) it from?

Phrasal Verbs with *Cut*

*Replace the words and expressions in **bold** with a phrasal verb from the box.*

cut off	cut in	cut down on	cut in	cut off	cut out	cut back

1. We will have to **spend less** on staff costs at work if we're to continue operating as normal..
2. We are trying to get him to **reduce** the number of cigarettes he smokes each day.
3. We were in the middle of a telephone conversation when we were suddenly **disconnected**.
4. I wish you wouldn't **interrupt** while I'm telling a story.
5. Did you see how the little white car **suddenly drove** in front of the black Audi?
6. She's decided to **stop eating** sweet things so as to lose weight.
7. He didn't pay his bill, so the company **stopped** his electricity.

Phrasal Verbs with *Do*

*Replace the words and expressions in **bold** with a phrasal verb from the box. Use your dictionary to check the position of the preposition and the object in each sentence.*

(could) do with	do up	do without	do away with	do in	do in	do up

1. The government are going to **get rid of** customs inspections.
2. Somebody decided to **kill** the gang boss and dump the body in the river.
3. I can't **fasten** this zip. Can you help me?
4. Why don't you buy that old cottage and **repair** it **so it is like new**?
5. After that long walk, I **need** a cup of tea.
6. Don't **hurt** your back digging the garden.
7. Plants can't **manage without** water.

Phrasal Verbs with *Get*

*Match the sentences in the left-hand column with those in the right hand column. Use the phrasal verbs in **bold** to help you.*

1. I'm trying to **get across** to the people in the office that they'll all have to work harder.	A. Really? How do you manage to live on that?
2. He was rude to the teacher, but **got away with** it somehow.	B. No. Her mother never recovered from the shock either.
3. How are you going to **get by** without a car?	C. She always thinks she's being criticized.
4. We **get by** on only £50 a week.	D. He needs someone to tell him to start working.
5. He'll have to **get down to** some hard work if he wants to pass the test.	E. Well, they've never been very friendly with each other.
6. They don't **get on** well at all.	F. That's great. I'm glad she's better at last.
7. She's **getting on** well at university.	G. Nothing naughty, I promise.
8. I want an excuse to **get out of** going to the office party.	H. Oh well, at least you've done it at last.
9. Kiki's **got over** her flu.	I. Have you had any luck making them understand?
10. She never **got over** the death of her father.	J. She always manages to persuade someone to do what she wants.
11. I only **got round to** sending my Christmas cards yesterday.	K. Yes, in fact he was very successful.
12. Jane **got round** the boss by giving him a bottle of wine.	L. Did you finally manage to speak to someone on the phone?
13. Did he **get through** his exams?	M. I don't believe he wasn't punished!
14. I tried to **get through to** the complaints department, but the line was busy.	N. It'll be difficult, but I'll manage.
15. Whatever did you **get up to** last night?	O. I always knew she'd do well.
16. She thinks she's being **got at**.	P. Typical! You're always trying to avoid doing something!

How many more phrasal verbs can you find that use get?

📖 You will find more expressions using get on pages 41-42.

Phrasal Verbs with *Give*

Complete the phrasal verbs in the sentences below with an appropriate preposition from the box.

in	out	away	up	off

1. He said he was French, but we didn't believe him as his accent gave him _____.
2. The company are giving _____ a free pocket calculator with every £10 purchase.
3. I can't use my watch because the battery has given _____.
4. She gave _____ presents to all the children.
5. She's trying to give _____ smoking.
6. The hijacker gave himself _____ to the police.
7. I didn't want to go to the cinema with the children, but they kept asking me so in the end I gave _____ and agreed to take them.
8. The fire in the factory gave _____ clouds of poisonous black smoke.

Phrasal Verbs with *Go*

Half of the phrasal verbs in the following sentences use the wrong preposition. Decide which ones are wrong and replace them with the correct preposition, which you will find in the other sentences.

1. The burglar alarm went **off** in the middle of the night, waking everybody up.
2. I think this fish has gone **down** - it stinks.
3. She went **about** her new boyfriend quite quickly when she discovered his nasty habits (☞habit).
4. The police investigating the murder don't have much to go **on**.
5. What on earth is going **out** here?
6. The fire went **on** and the room gradually became cold.
7. The bomb went **off** when there were still lots of people in the building.
8. The firm went out of business last week and their office has closed **off**.
9. The price of bread has gone **on** again. Last week it was 60p a loaf, now it's 70p.
10. They decided not to go **through with** their plans because of opposition from the neighbours.
11. Before you sign your contract (☞contract, def 1), you should go **over** it carefully with a solicitor.
12. We'd like to start our own company, but aren't sure how to go **off** it.
13. She said she had a new job but refused to go **into** details.
14. She went **up** speaking for two hours without stopping.
15. There wasn't enough ice cream to go **round**, so some of the children had chocolates instead.
16. Tony's going **out with** a girl from work. I think he's quite serious about her.

Phrasal Verbs with *Look*

Choose the correct phrasal verb in the following sentences.

1. Maureen isn't _____ taking her driving test. In fact, she's really worried about it.   **(looking over / looking forward to / looking into)**
2. Things haven't been good for a while, but at last they are _____. **(looking forward / looking down / looking up)**
3. We've got quite a nice view from our office. We _____ a park. **(look out over / look up / look down)**
4. Jane thinks she's better than people who haven't been to university and _____ them. **(looks up to / looks down on / looks out for)**
5. _____! The car is going backwards. **(Look out! / Look in! / Look over!)**
6. She has always admired intelligent men. For example, she _____ her professor and copies everything he does. **(looks down on / looks out for / looks up to)**
7. _____ me _____ when you're next in London - it will be nice to see you again. **(Look...forward / Look...up / Look...out)**
8. She _____ the figures (☞figure, def 1a) and they seemed to be OK. **(looked over / looked on / looked out for)**
9. I've asked the manager to _____ the question of staff holidays. **(look down on / look into / look on)**
10. Who's going to _____ your dog while you're away? **(look into / look out / look after)**
11. We're _____ new offices because ours are too small. **(looking down on / looking out for / looking up)**

Phrasal Verbs with *Make*

Look at the sentences on the left (which all use a phrasal verb with <u>make</u>) and match them with a possible situation on the right.

1. Can you **make out** the house in the dark? 2. I can't **make out** why he didn't come. 3. Don't worry. He **made up** the story about a man climbing into the house. 4. I can't **make up** my mind where to go this year. 5. He **made over** the property to his daughter last week. 6. I really don't know what to **make of** this letter she passed to me last night. 7. It's no use talking to him - his mind is **made up**.	A. Somebody has made a decision and won't change it. B. Somebody hasn't decided about their summer holiday yet. C. Somebody is puzzled (☞puzzled) about something they have been given. D. Somebody has just passed something to another person. E. Somebody is puzzled about his friend's absence from a party. F. Somebody has invented a tale (☞tale) to frighten their friends. G. Two people trying to find their way to a friend's place in the countryside at night.

☞*You will find more expressions in the dictionary under the entry for 'make'.*

Phrasal Verbs with *Pick*

Choose the most suitable definition for the phrasal verbs in the following sentences.

1. The manager is always picking on me.
    (A) The manager always criticizes me.
    (B) The manager tells me all his secrets.
    (C) The manager always chooses me when there is something important to do.

2. He picked out all the best fruit.
    (A) He threw all the best fruit in the bin.
    (B) He chose all the best fruit.
    (C) He gave the best fruit to other people.

3. She's a girl he picked up in a bar.
    (A) She's a girl he started a fight with in a bar.
    (B) She's a girl he criticized in a bar.
    (C) She's a girl he met by chance in a bar.

4. Business is picking up after the Christmas holiday.
    (A) Business is getting worse.
    (B) Business is continuing as normal.
    (C) Business is improving.

5. The car will pick you up at the hotel at 7 o'clock.
    (A) The car will collect you from the hotel.
    (B) The car will take you to the hotel.
    (C) The car will deliver something to you at the hotel.

6. He picked up some German when he was working in Berlin.
    (A) He met some German people.
    (B) He learnt some German without being taught.
    (C) He went to German lessons.

© Peter Collin Publishing, 1999
Based on the *English Dictionary for Students*, ISBN 1-901659-06-2

Phrasal Verbs with *Put*

Complete the story below with a suitable phrasal verb from the box.

put down	put up	put down	put off	put up with	put by
	put off	put through	put down		

I had managed to **1.**_____ some money for a holiday in Canada, but had **2.**_____ booking a flight until I had found a cheap one. Well, I eventually found a good deal with a local travel agency and, despite my friends who tried to **3.**_____ me _____ by saying that the agency was unreliable, I **4.**_____ a £50 deposit. The next day, I went back to the agency to collect the ticket it was closed. I went home and called the manager, but was **5.**_____ to an answering machine. Now, I'm a very tolerant person, and will **6.**_____ almost anything, but by this time I was furious, so I decided to go back to the travel agency. I got into my car, **7.**_____ my foot _____ and, to my horror, drove the car backwards into my living room window! I had accidentally reversed the car!; I suppose I could **8.**_____ the accident _____ to my temper and the fact that I wasn't thinking straight. Anyway, I had to get the builders in to repair the damage. Fortunately my friend has offered to **9.**_____ me _____ until the work is finished. And my holiday? I've spent all my holiday money on building repairs!

Phrasal Verbs with *Run*

Look at the questions in the left-hand column and match them with a suitable response in the right-hand column.

1. Why has the clock stopped?	A. I **ran across** it in an antiques shop in London.
2. Why is Molly in hospital?	B. Yes. He says he's going to **run for** Prime Minister one day!
3. Why did you come home by bus?	C. I'll **run** them **off** straight away.
4. Why's Rick looking so depressed?	D. Well, let's **run through** the guest list again to make sure.
5. Did the police interview him?	E. She was **run down** by a car on the Banbury Road.
6. Where did you find that beautiful vase?	F. They were **running up** debts of thousands of pounds each week.
7. Can you make me a few copies of this leaflet?	G. I think the battery has **run down**.
8. Have we forgotten to invite anyone to our wedding?	H. Not really. We **ran up against** a few unexpected difficulties.
9. You've met Mel Gibson haven't you?	I. The car **ran out of** petrol on my way back.
10. Why did the nightclub go out of business?	J. Yes. His statement **runs over** two pages.
11. Did your journey go well?	K. Penny **ran out on** him when he lost his job.
12. Is Bob very ambitious?	L. Yes, and I **ran into** him again last week in a cafe by the river.

Phrasal Verbs with *Set*

Look at the definitions for the phrasal verbs below and decide if they are TRUE or FALSE.

1. If you have just **set off** on a trip, this means you have just finished it.
2. If something **sets off** your asthma (☞asthma), this means it starts your asthma.
3. If you **set up** a company, this means that you have just closed your company down.
4. If you **set up** home, this means that you have just become homeless.
5. If you are **set up** by somebody, this means that they have deliberately deceived (☞deceive) you.
6. If your journey is **set back**, this means that it takes you longer than you expected.
7. If something has **set** you **back** financially, this means that you have just won some money.
8. If some bad weather has **set in**, this means that the bad weather has started and has become permanent.
9. If you **set aside** some money, this means that you spend it.
10. If you **set about** doing something, this means that you have just finished doing it.

Phrasal Verbs with *Take*

Which definition, A, B or C, most accurately explains each sentence on the left.

1. Carol **takes after** her mother

    A. Carol does everything for her mother
    B. Carol looks like her mother.
    C. Carol is unkind to her mother.

2. Thousands of people were **taken in** by the advertisement

    A. Thousands of people ignored the advertisement
    B. Thousands of people were used to make the advertisement
    C. Thousands of people were deceived by the advertisement

3. She didn't **take in** anything you said.

    A. She didn't understand anything you said.
    B. She didn't do anything you told her to.
    C. She didn't hear you.

4. Sales **took off** after the TV commercial.

    A. Sales started to go down after the commercial.
    B. Sales started to rise fast after the commercial.
    C. Sales stayed the same after the commercial.

5. Miss Black **took over** from Mr Jones.

    A. Mr Jones started doing Miss Black's job.
    B. Miss Black and Mr Jones worked together.
    C. Miss Black started doing Mr Jones' job.

6. She decided to **take up** long-distance running

    A. She decided to stop long-distance running.
    B. She decided to try to improve her long-distance running ability.
    C. She decided to start long-distance running.

7. We need to **take on** more staff.

    A. We need to dismiss more staff.
    B. We need to employ more staff.
    C. We need to pay our staff more.

Most of the phrasal verbs above can have more than one definition. The PCP English Dictionary for Students lists 3 phrasal verbs which use take with 37 definitions. How many can you think of without looking at the dictionary?

Phrasal Verbs with *Turn*

Match the phrasal verbs on the left with an item they can be used with on the right. Most of the verbs can be used with more than one item.

| turn down |
| turn into |
| turn out |
| turn away |
| turn off |
| turn over |
| turn up |
| turn on |

cars (in a factory)   the page of a book   a road   a job   people from a house because they haven't paid the rent   a radio   a lost child   the television   guests at a party   the heat on a cooker   money   a light   people from a restaurant because it is full   a television   applicants for a job

Other Phrasal Verbs

Rewrite the following sentences using a phrasal verb from the box. You will need to change the verb form in most of the sentences.

keep on   face up to   let down   carry out   call off   hold up   wear out   break up   pull out
hold on (*or* hang on)   carry on   fall behind   split up   pull off   break down   show off   fall out
count on   end up   work out   call on   let off   break into   pull up   pull through   fall through
wear out   show up   wear off   sort out

1. The lift has stopped working again.
2. I'm trying to calculate if we've sold more this year than last year.
3. After walking across the USA, his boots were broken and useless.
4. The effects of the drug disappeared after a few hours.
5. She made herself very tired looking after the old lady.
6. She recovered, thanks to the help of the specialists.
7. Did you settle the problem of the hotel bill?
8. They had an argument and started to live apart.
9. We invited all our friends to the picnic but it rained and only five of them came.
10. A car stopped and the driver asked me if I wanted a lift.
11. Our Australian partners stopped being a part of the deal at the last moment.
12. The terrorists fired guns in the street.
13. The people I asked to speak at the meeting didn't help me even though I expected them to.
14. It will be marvellous if we are successful.
15. The cars continued moving even though the road was covered with snow.
16. The planes were delayed by fog.
17. Wait a moment, I'll get my umbrella.
18. Don't watch her dancing like that - she's just showing how much better than other people she thinks she is.
19. Our planned holiday in Spain didn't take place because we had too much work at the office.
20. After the movie, we all finished the evening at my girlfriend's flat.
21. Doctors did some tests on the patients.
22. They continued working even though the office was on fire.
23. He was late with his mortgage (☞mortgage, def 1b) repayments.
24. She visited her mother to see how she was.
25. The oil tanker was coming to pieces on the rocks.
26. They had an argument over the bill for the drinks.
27. He had to accept the unpleasant fact that he was never going to be rich.
28. He decided not to go ahead with the visit to the museum.
29. Can I be sure that you will help wash the dishes?
30. Burglars used force to get into the office during the night.

Based on the *English Dictionary for Students*, ISBN 1-901659-06-2

Phrasal Verbs Test

Complete the following sentences with a verb / preposition combination from the two boxes. You will need to change the verb form in most of the sentences. All of the phrasal verbs have appeared on the last eight pages.

look	pick	get	set	make	cut	run
pick	go	turn	give	take	come	put
		break	do			

down	away	into	forward	through	off
up	across	in	with	by	back	after
		over	on			

1.   We _____ a little restaurant when we were out walking.
2.   I'm really thirsty. I could _____ a nice cold drink.
3.   Now that winter has _____, we can expect to spend more money on heating bills.
4.   When the manager retired, I _____ his job.
5.   He _____ me _____ outside the hotel and drove me to the airport.
6.   We _____ some money each month for a holiday.
7.   Claudia _____ her aunt. They look so similar.
8.   They offered me a job, but I _____ it _____ .
9.   The bomb _____ at midnight, so fortunately the building was empty.
10. We were in the middle of a telephone conversation when we were suddenly _____ .
11. The first thing he did when he opened the exam paper was to _____ all the questions.
12. The exam has been _____ . It's now on Thursday instead of Monday.
13. I managed to _____ some Japanese while I was working in Tokyo.
14. Bob is trying to _____ smoking.
15. (On the phone) Good morning. can you _____ me _____ to the manager?
16. Guess who I _____ last night? Laurence Bailey! Remember him?
17. I've _____ my mind and nothing will change it!
18. We told him to shut up, but he _____ speaking.
19. I _____ to hearing from you soon.
20. We are trying to get him to _____ on the number of cigarettes he smokes.
21. Living in the country, I can't _____ without a car.
22. Thieves _____ the shop and stole over £30,000.
23. He _____ a story about a ghost in the attic - of course, nobody believed him.
24. I can't _____ these buttons. can you help me?
25. Her grandparents _____ her while her parents were away.
26. Our rent has _____ from £350 to £400.
27. We're _____ a free camera to anyone who spends more than £100.
28. My car has _____ again. I'll have to take it to the garage.
29. The message _____ on the radio this morning.
30. Olivia is _____ well in her new job.
31. The restaurant had to _____ customers _____ because it was full.

© Peter Collin Publishing, 1999
Based on the English Dictionary for Students, ISBN 1-901659-06-2

Phonetic Symbols

PROFILE
- Phonetic symbols are symbols which show you how a word is pronounced.
- There are 48 phonetic symbols used throughout your dictionary. You will find a complete list of these symbols, together with sample words, at the beginning of the dictionary.
- The phonetic symbols appear after each main entry in the dictionary.

> **lie**[lai] **1** *verb* **(a)** to say something which is not true; *she was lying when she said she had been at home all evening; he lied about the accident to the headmaster* (NOTE:in this meaning: **lying-lied**) **(b)** to be in a flat position; to be situated; *six soldiers lay dead on the ground; the dog spends the evening lying in front of*

- Often in English, one letter can be pronounced in more than one way, depending on the word it is being used in. This is why it is important you familiarise yourself with the phonetic symbols in your dictionary.
- Some letters change their pronunciation when the word they are in is used with other words (eg, 'Do you want **to** go to the cinema?' 'No, I don't want **to**'.)

PRACTICE 1
Read the text below and match the letters in bold with the appropriate phonetic symbols in the grid. Write the words in the grid. (Two of the phonetic symbols are not featured in the text).

ST. CLARE'S INTERNATIONAL COLLEGE, OXFORD
RULES FOR A BETTER STUDYING ENVIRONMENT

It can sometimes be difficult living and studying in a strange country. However, if you pay attention to the following cultural tips, your stay in Oxford will be more pleasant and en**j**oyable for you and for those around you.

1. British people are always saying *please*, **th**ank *you* and *sorry*. These are probably the most important words in **our** language! Practise them in the classroom and use **th**em whenever **y**ou can!
2. Students at St. Clare's **c**ome from all over the world. You should be sensitive to those ar**ou**nd you; remember that **n**ot everyone comes from the same cultural background as you.
3. You **sh**ould speak English at all times, especially if you are in a mixed-nationality gr**ou**p. After all, that is the reason you are h**er**e!
4. St. Clare's is in a residential district of Oxford. Please respect our neighbours by keeping n**oi**se to a minimum, especially in the evenings and at nigh**t**.
5. Try to be aw**are** of the people around you. For example, don't block the pavements so that other people have to **w**alk into the road.
6. Try to **h**elp people if they have problems. For example, the next time you see your poor, hardworking t**ea**cher trying to open the door with a handful of b**oo**ks, be nice and hold the d**oo**r open for them!
7. Don't **thr**ow your cigarette ends and chewing gum on the floor. Try to **k**eep our **c**ollege tidy.
8. Don't criti**c**ize or make fun of other people, especially if they don't speak English as well as you.
9. Don't **c**omplain all the time - remember that nobody or nothi**ng** is perfect!
10. Make the most of your leisure time to explore your environment. The Student Activities Officer will help you if you want to h**ire** a car, book a hotel room or go on a guided tour. And of course, don't forget our half-term trip to Lo**ch** Ness and the Scottish Highlands.
11. Above all, have a good time!

Put the words in the text above and on the previous page into their appropriate space in the table below.

PRACTICE 2

Pronunciation pairs. Match the words in the left hand column with those in the right hand column based on the pronunciation of the letters and groups of letters in **bold**. These letters should have the same pronunciation.

full catch **a**nchor **c**ello **zoo** **ha**re bean
course sun mon**ey** **f**un b**oy**s **f**low **tie** m**ou**se
crate **th**rough **la**rge **c**lay **bee**r

abroad now h**oi**st b**oa**t h**u**m b**ea**r b**uy**
l**ose** **ch**eers **ph**oney **ch**oose **c**an't **ear**
pl**a**te gr**ea**t p**ee**k w**oo**d **c**ertain h**a**ll ke**ttle**

Odd One Out

PROFILE

- Students often complain that many letters and combinations of letters in English do not follow any rules of pronunciation. For example, the combination of *-ough* can be pronounced in 5 ways. Look these words up in your dictionary and notice how *-ough* is pronounced in each word:

through   dough   cough   tough   bough.

Use your dictionary to find out which of the words on the right does not rhyme (☞rhyme, def 2) with the word on the left.

1. heard	word bird beard third
2. dead	bed bead said thread
3. meat	seat suite threat treat
4. bear	pear there fear stare
5. steak	beak bake break stake
6. worse	purse nurse horse hearse
7. weight	wait hate straight height
8. thumb	come sum home some
9. tomb	womb loom bomb boom
10. sew	few so low show
11. shown	phone town loan tone
12. fear	beer dear leer bear
13. should	mould could wood good
14. please	freeze cheese peace tease
15. paid	afraid made weighed said
16. soul	goal hole whole foul
17. tool	pool wool cool fool
18. won	son sun one gone
19. cart	thwart start part chart
20. catch	match latch batch watch
21. loose	choose moose juice sluice
22. wonder	blunder thunder wander plunder
23. walk	work talk pork cork
24. fruit	shoot loot boot foot
25. chase	vase face lace race

85

Based on the *English Dictionary for Students*, ISBN 1-901659-06-2

Stress

PROFILE

- All words which have more than one syllable (☞syllable) have one syllable which is spoken more strongly than the others. This is called *stress*.
- It is important to stress a word correctly, otherwise it can be difficult to understand what you are saying.
- In your dictionary, stress has been indicated by a main stress mark ('), but these are only guides as the stress of the word may be changed according to its position in the sentence.
- Often, when words change their form, the position of the stress changes and this can sometimes change other aspects of the pronunciation. Look up these words in your dictionary and notice how, as the stress changes, so does the pronunciation of the vowels.

photograph   photography   photographic

- Some words can be both nouns and verbs without changing their form. Nouns are often stressed on their first syllable. Verbs are often stressed on their second syllable. Sometimes, other aspects of the pronunciation are different. Look up these words in your dictionary to find out if, as the stress changes, so does the pronunciation of the vowel.

record (as a noun)   record (as a verb)
produce (as a noun)   produce (as a verb)
increase (as a noun)   increase (as a verb)

Look up these words in your dictionary to find out (a) if the stress changes its position and (b) if any of the vowels in **bold** are pronounced differently as a result.

1. employ employee	15. sympathy sympathise sympathetic
2. present (noun) present (verb)	16. luxury luxurious
3. rebel (noun) rebel (verb)	17. **o**rigin original
4. answer (noun) answer (verb)	18. guitar guitarist
5. advertise advertisement	19. obscene obscenity
6. disagree disagreement	20. massage (noun) massage (verb)
7. depart departure	21. electric electricity
8. **u**nfortunate unfortunately	22. decorate decorator
9. economics economise	23. conduct (noun) conduct (verb)
10. discuss discussion	24. decrease (noun) decrease (verb)
11. suspect (noun) suspect (verb)	25. fortune fortunate fortunately
12. operate operator operation	26. contact (noun) contact (verb)
13. indicate indicator indication	27. attempt (noun) attempt (verb)
14. compute computer	28. decide decision

© Peter Collin Publishing, 1999
Based on the *English Dictionary for Students*, ISBN 1-901659-06-2

Now put the words above into the table on the previous page according to the position of the stress. The symbol ◆ shows the position of the stress.

○◆ (eg, pro**duce** (verb))	◆○ (eg, **produce** (noun))
◆○○ (eg, **pho**tograph)	○◆○ (eg, esta**bli**sh)
○○◆ (eg, discon**tent**)	◆○○○ (eg, **Irish**woman)
○◆○○ (eg, pho**to**graphy)	○○◆○ (eg, re-es**tab**lish)
○○◆○○ (eg, unpro**noun**cable)	○◆○○○ (eg, un**ques**tionable)

Use your dictionary to find more examples to put into the table.

Based on the *English Dictionary for Students*, ISBN 1-901659-06-2

Same Spelling / Same pronunciation / Different meaning

PROFILE
A lot of English words can have the same spelling, the same pronunciation, but more than one meaning.

Look at this example from the dictionary. *Lie*, as a verb, has two meanings. As a noun it has one meaning.

> **lie**[lai] **1** *verb* **(a)** to say something which is not true; *she was lying when she said she had been at home all evening; he lied about the accident to the headmaster* (NOTE: in this meaning: **lying-lied**) **(b)** to be in a flat position; to be situated; *six soldiers lay dead on the ground; the dog spends the evening lying in front of the fire; there were bits of paper and cigarette packets lying all over the pavement; the city of Quito lies near the equator;* **to lie in wait for someone** = to hide and wait for someone to come so as to attack him (NOTE: in this meaning: **lying - lay**[lel]- **has lain**[leln]) **2** *noun* something which is not true; *that's a lie! - don't believe what he says; someone has been telling lies about her.*

PUNS
A pun is a joke where one word, which has the same spelling and pronunciation, can have two meanings.
Look at these puns and use your dictionary to help you choose the appropriate word from the box to complete the sentences.

call	charge	count	bright	patient	change	beat	atmosphere	bar	horns

1. Why did the teacher wear sunglasses?
   Because his students were so ....

2. Jim has just swallowed some coins!
   Really? I haven't noticed any .... in him.

3. Why should you never hold a party on the moon?
   Because there's not much ....

4. Policeman: I'm arresting you.
   Man: What's the .... ?
   Policeman: Nothing. It's free.

5. A man walked into a .... Ouch! It was an iron ....

6. Why do cows wear bells?
   In case their .... don't work.

7. The cook in our school is really cruel.
   How do you know?
   Yesterday I saw him .... some eggs.

8. What did one pocket calculator say to the other?
   You can always .... on me.

9. Man: Doctor, please help me! Every day I become shorter.
   Doctor: I'm afraid you'll have to be a little ....

10. .... me a taxi.
    OK. You're a taxi.

© Peter Collin Publishing, 1999
Based on the *English Dictionary for Students*, ISBN 1-901659-06-2

WORDSEARCH

Look at the definitions below and find the words that match them in the box. Then look in your dictionary to see if these words have any other meanings.

1. a round metal container for food / a modal verb (📖 Glossary, page 2)
2. a ridge of water on the surface of the sea, a lake or a river / to move up and down in the wind.
3. a hole in the ground where a dead person is buried / important or worrying
4. nasty or unpleasant / to show or represent
5. quite cold / not enthusiastic
6. a business which holds money for its clients / the land along the side of a river
7. a large bus for travelling long distances / a person who trains sportsmen, etc.
8. a round shape of metal / to make a sound with a bell.
9. brightness, the opposite of darkness / not heavy
10. a game between two teams / a small piece of wood or cardboard which catches fire when you rub it against a rough surface.

c	a	b	m	a	t	c	h	c	d
w	a	v	e	j	i	h	g	f	e
k	l	n	a	n	p	c	o	o	l
x	y	z	n	v	u	t	s	r	q
a	l	i	g	h	t	b	d	b	c
r	p	n	g	o	h	l	k	a	j
s	t	z	r	c	x	r	i	n	g
j	u	l	a	i	e	t	k	k	l
o	f	o	v	x	n	h	l	o	p
c	c	l	e	b	c	n	k	p	q

Based on the *English Dictionary for Students*, ISBN 1-901659-06-2

Different spelling / Same pronunciation / Different meaning

PROFILE

- A lot of English words can have the same pronunciation, but a different spelling and more than one meaning.

Look at these examples from the dictionary.

> **sea** [si:] *noun* **(a)** area of salt water between continents or islands, but not as large as an ocean; *swimming in the sea is more exciting than swimming in a river; the*

> **see**[si:] **1** *verb* **(a)** to use your eyes to notice; *can you see that tree in the distance?; they say eating carrots help you see in the dark; we ran because we could see the bus coming; I have never seen a badger before*

1. Look at these sentences and choose the correct word to fill the gaps. Both options have the same pronunciation but a different meaning.

1. **dear / deer**
    The children saw a _____ in the park.

2. **break / brake**
    He managed to stop the car safely using the hand _____ .

3. **fête / fate**
    They met by chance in a bar and got married - it must have been _____ .

4. **great / grate**
    Finally, _____ some parmesan cheese and put it on your pasta.

5. **male / mail**
    My secretary opens my _____ as soon as it arrives.

6. **naval / navel**
    He comes from a _____ family; all his brothers are sailors.

7. **pain / pane**
    If you have a _____ in the chest, you should see a doctor.

8. **paste / paced**
    He _____ backwards and forwards in front of the door.

9. **sail / sale**
    The _____ of the house produced £200,000.

10. **steaks / stakes**
    They hammered _____ into the ground to put up a wire fence.

11. **stationery / stationary**
    The letter was typed on his office _____ .

12. **suede / swayed**
    He was wearing blue _____ shoes.

13. **tail / tale**
    She told the children a _____ of princesses and wicked fairies.

14. **whale / wail**
    She sat down and started to _____ when she read the news.

15. **waist / waste**
    She measures 32 inches around the _____ .

2. Read the story below. There are 17 words in the story which are *pronounced* correctly but are *spelt* incorrectly. Find them and correct them. Use your dictionary to help you.

KING OF THE JUNGLE

Larry the lion was very fierce and all the other animals in the jungle were afraid of him. He had always bean very proud of this fact.

One day, while he was out walking, who should he meat but Morris the monkey. Larry stopped him before he could flea.
"Who's the King of the jungle, little monkey?" asked Larry.

"Uh, ewe are." replied Morris the monkey, and quickly ran away, putting several hundred meters between himself and Larry.

Larry continued walking until he came across Bert the bare.

"Hey you! Who's the King of the jungle?" demanded Larry.

"You are, so I here," replied Bert, cautiously backing into the bushes.

Feeling very pleased with himself, Larry continued walking until he bumped into Dave the dear. Larry court him by the antlers before he could escape

"Who's the King of the jungle?" asked Larry?

"You're such a well-bread animal, it must be you," wined Dave. This pleased Larry and he aloud Dave to walk away. He carried on walking until he sore Gary the gorilla sitting in his tree.

"Hey you, ugly, who's the King of the jungle?" asked Larry.

Gary ignored him, so Larry let out a deafening raw.

"I said, who's the King of the jungle, you stupid gorilla?"

Gary climbed down from his tree, walked up to Larry, hit him over the head with a piece of would, picked him up, through him on the ground and jumped up and down on him. He then climbed back into his tree.

Larry looked up at him and said "All right. There's no need to get angry just because you don't no the answer"

Record Sheets

Word forms record sheet

Photocopy and use this sheet to keep a record of different word forms. You will not need to use all of the spaces on the sheet. Two examples have been given.

Verb 1	Verb 2	Adjective 1	Adjective 2	Adjective 3	Noun 1	Noun 2
excite	::::::::::::::::	exciting	excited	excitable	excitement	::::::::::::::
obey	disobey	obedient	disobedient	:::::::::::::::	obedience	disobedience

© Peter Collin Publishing, 1999
Based on the *English Dictionary for Students*, ISBN 1-901659-06-2

Vocabulary record sheet

TOPIC:	

WORD OR EXPRESSION	DEFINITION	SAMPLE SENTENCE(S)

Continue onto a new page if you need to add more words and expressions to your list

Phrasal verb record sheet

MAIN VERB:

PHRASAL VERB	DEFINITION	SAMPLE SENTENCE(S)

Continue onto a new page if you need to add more phrasal verbs to your list

© Peter Collin Publishing, 1999
Based on the *English Dictionary for Students*, ISBN 1-901659-06-2

Answer Key

⇩3 Grammatical Function. Pages 6 - 7

PRACTICE A

deliberate has 2 grammatical functions (a verb and an adjective)
degenerate has 3 functions (an adjective, a verb and a noun)
stock has 3 functions (a noun, a verb and an adjective)
straight has 3 functions (an adjective, an adverb and a noun)
behind has 3 functions (a preposition, an adverb and a noun)

PRACTICE B

and = conjunction   happy = adjective   sadly = adverb   come = verb   London = proper noun   into = preposition   me = pronoun   the = article   mine = object pronoun

PRACTICE C

1. Look   2. in   3. easily   4. I / this / that   5. but   6. you   7. useful

⇩4 Definition. Page 7

look has 6 definitions   *invent* has 2 definitions
iron has 5 definitions   *triangle* has 2 definitions
make has 7 definitions   *do* has 18 definitions

⇩5 Derivatives. Page 8

act has 8 derivatives (acting / action / activate / active / actively / activist / activity / actor (actress))
agree has 3 derivatives (agreeable / agreed / agreement)
bore has 3 derivatives (boredom / boring / bored)
continue has 8 derivatives (continual / continually / continuance / continuation / continuing / continuous / continuously / continuum)
satisfy has 4 derivatives (satisfaction / satisfactory / satisfied / satisfying)
hope has 5 derivatives (hoped-for / hopeful / hopefully / hopeless / hopelessly)
decide has 2 derivatives (decided / decidely)

⇩6 Phrasal Verbs. Page 8

take off has 6 definitions   *cut in* has 2 definitions
do in has 2 definitions   *get on* has 5 definitions
go off has 5 definitions   *make up* has 5 definitions
set up has 2 definitions

⇩ 7 Compound Words. Page 8

birthday party   lie in   software   trade union   hardware / hardback   takeover   junk food
alarm clock   police station   lifejacket

⇩ 8 Idioms, Colloquialisms, Slang Expressions And Proverbs. Page 9

If someone offered you a *fag*, you would either refuse or accept one. A fag is a cigarette in British-English
A bird in the hand is worth two in the bush means that you should be satisfied with what you have got, rather than hope for something better which may never come.
A *wet blanket* is a miserable person who spoils an activity.
If you were *on cloud nine*, you would feel very happy.
If you *slept like a log*, you slept well.
If your bank account is *in the red*, you owe your bank money because you have spent more than the amount that was in the account.

⇩ Review. Page 10

1. looking glass / lookalike
2. look
3. seeing something with your eyes / the way someone or something appears / searching for something / turn your eyes towards something, etc.
4. look back

5. completely / completion
6. look someone in the eye
7. noun / verb, etc.
8. [luk], etc
9. don't look a gift horse in the mouth

⇩ Plural Forms. Page 11

crisis = crises   wife = wives   fish = fish   potato = potatoes   tomato = tomatoes
knife = knives   phenomenon = phenomena   bacterium = bacteria   child = children
man = men   woman = women   patch = patches   scarf = scarves   half = halves
wolf = wolves

⇩ Grammatical, Cultural And Other Background Information. Page 11

PRACTICE A
You will find the answers to these questions under the following main words in the dictionary:
1. judge   2. cricket   3. pepperpot   4. shake hands   5. breakfast   6. November   7. ID (card)   8. cracker

PRACTICE B
You will find the answers to these questions under the following main words in the dictionary:
1. superlative   2. auxiliary verb   3. apostrophe   4. modal verb

⇩ British And American English. Page 12

candy = American   cupboard = British   elevator = American   janitor = American
faucet = American   pavement = British and American (although the meaning is different)
store = American   expressway = American

⇩ Irregular Verbs And Other Information. Page 12

spin = spun / spun
overdo = overdid / overdone
burn, dream, dwell and *learn* can be either regular or irregular verbs
0171-921-3567 is spoken *oh one seven one. nine two one. three five six seven.*
£27.36 is spoken *twenty one pounds (and) thirty six (pence)*
The year *1998* is spoken *nineteen ninety eight*
The year *2000* is spoken *two thousand*
2.1.98 in Britain is the *second of January* 1998. In the USA it's the *first of February* 1998.
If it is midday in London, it is 2 o'clock in the afternoon in Cairo, the same in Athens, and 8 o'clock in the evening in Singapore.
The international telephone code for the United Kingdom is 44
The international telephone code for Spain is 34

⇩ Nouns Formed From Verbs And Adjectives (Abstract Nouns). Pages 13-14

B. Dictionary practice.
1. ☞ Dictionary page 33
2. The noun for *argue* is *argument*
3. The noun ends with *-ment*
4. The letter *e* is removed from *argue*.

NOUNS FORMED FROM VERBS
-ment: excitement astonishment treatment development amazement embarrassment announcement arrangement argument
-ion: discussion satisfaction repetition permission completion
-ation: expectation admiration cancellation variation (or variety) hesitation organization pronunciation formation
Others: preference death birth insistence disappearance obedience loss resistance behaviour (USA = behavior) pleasure signature approval complaint failure persistence survival breakage belief success proof arrival assistance choice performance receipt discovery qualification laughter

PRACTICE
1. performance   2. excitement   3. pronunciation   4. birth   5. qualifications   6. argument
7. embarrassment   8. discovery   9. amazement   10. disappearance

NOUNS FORMED FROM ADJECTIVES
-ity: maturity similarity stupidity popularity rarity validity purity probability possibility responsibility equality necessity reliability superiority inferiority
-ence: violence patience insolence confidence intelligence

-ness: happiness illness foolishness loneliness whiteness selfishness
Others: heat relevance bravery (or courage) boredom justice loyalty realism pessimism optimism accuracy sympathy warmth anger width certainty pride
anxiety hunger safety strength thirst length depth height honesty truth

PRACTICE
1. heat   2. strength   3. truth   4. violence   5. hunger   6. patience   7. bravery
8. honesty   9. happiness   10. illness

⇩ Compound Words. Page 15

B. Dictionary practice
1. ☞ Dictionary page 68
2. There are 4 compound words: birthday cake, birthday card, birthday party, birthday presents.
3. They are written as two words.
4. ☞ Dictionary pages 339-340
5. There are 21 compound words: half-brother, half-day, half-dollar, half-dozen (or half a dozen), half-empty, half-full, half-hearted, half-holiday, half-hour, half-hourly, half-mast, half past, half price, half-sister, half-staff, half-term, half-time, halfway, halfwit, half-year, half-yearly.
6. 2 are written as one word, 2 are written as two words, the rest are hyphenated.
7. ☞ Dictionary page 822.
8. There are 11 compound words: trade price, trade in, trade-in, trademark (or trade name), trade off, trade-off, trade on, trader, tradesman, trade union (or trades union), trade unionist. (Trades Union Congress is not a compound word - it is the name of an organization)
9. 1 is written as one word, 2 are hyphenated and the rest are written as two words.

1.   COMPOUND NOUNS
food poisoning   homework   fairy story   moonlight   bookmark   bookcase   hair dryer
income tax   air pollution   toothpaste   traffic pollution   traffic lights   football boots
race relations   table tennis   parking meter   water pollution   water basin   water meter
timetable   stamp collection   airline pilot   sunlight   sunglasses   question mark   shoelaces

1. fairy story   2. traffic lights   3. sunlight   4. Air pollution   5. Race relations   6. income tax
7. food poisoning   8. shoelaces   9. parking meter   10. timetable

2.   COMPOUND ADJECTIVES
world-famous   short-sighted   sun-tanned   well-off or well-made   run-down   absent-minded   fair-haired   hard-up   eye-catching   hand-made   three-star

1. three star   2. world-famous   3. sun-tanned   4. short-sighted   5. well-made   6. eye-catching   7. hand-made   8. run-down
9. well-off   10. absent-minded

⇩ Adjectives Formed From Verbs. Page 16

B. Dictionary practice

-ive	-al	-ous	-able	-ing	-ful	-ed
active	**continual**	**continuous**	admirable	**frightening**	useful	**frightened**

1. active   2. admirable   3. agreeable   4. apologetic   5. boring   6. bored   7. careful
8. comparable   9. competitive   10. constructive   11. continual   12. continuous
13. creative   14. decisive   15. dependable   16. doubtful   17. excitable   18. exciting
19. excited   20. hopeful   21. preferable   22. recognizable   23. satisfying
24. suspicious   25. useful   26. variable

⇩ Opposites Of Adjectives. Pages 17-18

B. Dictionary practice
1. Incorrect. The adjective is **dis**agreeable
2. Correct
3. Correct
4. Incorrect. The adjective is **un**attractive
5. Incorrect. The adjective is **il**logical
6. Correct

dis-: disadvantaged dissatisfied disagreeable discontented dishonest disinclined disobedient
il-: illegal illegitimate illiterate illogical

im-: immortal immoral impure impossible immature immobile impatient imperfect improper impersonal
in-: incomplete inaccurate inadequate incurable incompetent incorrect
ir-: irrational irregular irresolute irresponsible irreplaceable irrelevant irresistible
un-: unqualified unavoidable unconscious unacceptable unattractive unfair unconvincing uneven unmarried
unwelcome uncomfortable unfashionable unlimited uncertain unbelievable

1. unacceptable 2. irreplaceable 3. unfair 4. impatient 5. illegal 6. unlimited
7. disobedient 8. immature 9. illiterate 10. uncertain 11. disadvantaged 12. irresistible
13. unconscious 14. dishonest 15. irresponsible

⇩ Opposites Of Verbs. Page 19

PROFILE
B. Dictionary practice
1. Incorrect. The verb is **dis**appeared.
2. Incorrect. The verb is **mis**represented.
3. Incorrect. The verb is **un**fastened.

1. misbehaves 2. unpacking 3. unwrapping 4. disobey 5. misused 6. disapproves 7. mispronounce 8. disprove
9. dislike 10. unlock 11. disqualified 12. unfolded 13. discontinued 14. misplaced 15. disconnected

---

⇩ Nouns Formed From Nouns And Verbs. Page 20

build = builder science = scientist design = designer advise = advisor labour = labourer chemistry = chemist study
= student rob = robber law = lawyer crime = criminal write = writer terror = terrorist survive = survivor library =
librarian manage = manager politics = politician own = owner collect = collector direct = director
guitar = guitarist electric = electrician teach = teacher operate = operator art = artist
piano = pianist

⇩ Modified Words. Page 21

1. anti-climax 2. foresee 3. post-holiday 4. under-estimate 5. pro-European 6. antisocial 7. undergraduates
8. forearmed 9. anticlockwise 10. forewarned 11. foresee 12. overdue 13. undermined 14. pre-Christmas
15. overestimated

⇩ Abbreviations. Pages 22-23

1. ORGANIZATIONS AND PEOPLE
A. 1. UN (United Nations) 2. WHO (World Health Organisation) 3. BBC (British Broadcasting Corporation) 4. CID
(Criminal Investigation Department) 5. CIA (Central Intelligence Agency) 6. FBI (Federal Bureau of Investigation) 7. EU
(European Union) 8. NHS (National Health Service) 9. AA (Automobile Association) 10. OPEC (Organization of
Petroleum Exporting Countries) 11. UK (United Kingdom) 12. MP (Member of Parliament) 13. MEP (Member of the
European Parliament) 14. PC (Police Constable) 15. VIP (Very important person)

B. 1. MP 2. MEP 3. EU 4. WHO 5. UN 6. OPEC 7. BBC 8. CID 9. FBI 10. AA

2. COMMON ABBREVIATIONS
1. b 2. a 3. c 4. c 5. a 6. c 7. b 8. c

⇩ Accommodation. Pages 24-25

1. **VERBS**
1. decorate 2. rent 3. extend 4. demolish 5. evict 6. lease 7. let 8. move in
The word in the shaded vertical strip is *renovate*.

2. **NOUNS AND ADJECTIVES**
A. 1. terraced house 2. prison cell 3. hospital ward 4. castle 5. caravan 6. cottage
7. mansion 8. detached house 9. semi-detached house 10. palace 11. bungalow
12. houseboat 13. flat (in the USA = *apartment*) 14. barracks (used by soldiers)

B. (In order, top to bottom):
television aerial / chimney / roof / attic / roof gutter / second floor / first floor / ground floor / cellar
(NB: In the USA, the ground floor is called the first floor, the first floor is the second floor and so on. A television *aerial* in
the USA is a television *antenna*
The word *basement* can sometimes be used instead of *cellar*. In Britain, some people live in *basement flats*).

3. IDIOMS, COLLOQUIALISMS AND OTHER EXPRESSIONS
1.FALSE 2.FALSE 3.TRUE 4.FALSE (note the difference in meaning in American English) 5.TRUE 6.TRUE
7.FALSE 8.TRUE 9.FALSE

⇩ British and American English. Pages 26-27

1. SPELLING

British English	American English
centre	center
traveller	traveler
colour	color
dialogue	dialog

2. VOCABULARY
A. 1A. American 1B. British 2A. British 2B. American 3A. American 3B. British
4A. British 4B. American

B. 1. tap = faucet 2. lawyer = attorney 3. rubber = eraser (NB Beware! a *rubber* in the USA is a contraceptive sheath)
4. motorway = expressway (the word *freeway* can also be used) 5. autumn = fall 6. dustbin = garbage can 7.
interval = intermission 8. railway = railroad 9. rise = raise 10. toilet = rest room (in public places only. In a
private residence, Americans say *bathroom*) 11. pavement = sidewalk (In the USA, the *pavement* is the surface of
the road) 12. cooker = stove 13. holiday = vacation (In the USA, a *holiday* is a day off work to celebrate a
national event such as Thanksgiving or Christmas) 14. garden = yard 15. play truant = play hookey 16. bill =
check

⇩ Cars And Driving. Pages 28-29

1. NOUNS
A.
Exterior:
1. windscreen 2. bonnet 3. headlights 4. tyre 5. aerial 6. radiator grill 7. indicators 8. mirrors 9. boot
10. bumper 11. number plate

Interior:
1. horn 2. speedometer 3. tax disc 4. mirror 5. fuel gauge 6. steering wheel 7. accelerator 8. brake pedal
9. clutch pedal 10. handbrake 11. gear lever 12. glove compartment

B. Use your PCP *English Dictionary for Students* to find the differences.

2. VERBS
1. adjust 2. started up 3. stalled 4. fasten 5. release 6. pulled away 7. check 8. crashed / smashed 9. sounded
10. skidded 11. swerve 12. accelerated 13. braked 14. crashed / smashed 15. overtake 16. indicate 17. reverse

3. IDIOMS, COLLOQUIALISMS AND OTHER EXPRESSIONS
Use your PCP English Dictionary for Students to look up the meanings of the words and expressions in bold.

⇩ Clothes. Pages 30-31

1. VERBS
1. C 2. C 3. A 4. B 5. A 6. B 7. C 8. B 9. B 10. A 11. A 12. B

2. NOUNS AND ADJECTIVES
A.
1. Bob 2. Jim 3. Miranda 4. Jim 5. Miranda 6. Tony 7. Miranda 8. Miranda 9. Tony 10. Mr Johnson
11. Tony 12. Jenny 13. Jenny 14. Bob 15. Tony 16. Jenny 17. Bob 18. Bob 19. Bob 20. Tony 21. Tony

B. 1. buckle 2. sleeve 3. pocket 4. button 5. seam 6. lace (usually used in the plural, *laces*) 7. collar 8. cuff

3. IDIOMS, COLLOQUIALISMS AND OTHER EXPRESSIONS
secretly = up her sleeve sacked him = gave him the boot nonsense = talking through his hat had a plan which he was
keeping secret = was keeping something up his sleeve
try to do better = pull his socks up place = shoes admire = take my hat off to
on a small amount of money = on a shoestring be quiet = belt up wearing his very best clothes = dressed up to the nines
secret = under his hat hit her hard = give her a sock on the jaw worked closely = been hand in glove

1. now / actually 2. advice / advise 3. effect / affect 4. yet / already 5. afraid of / worried about 6. prevent / avoid 7. beside / besides 8. fetch / bring 9. chance / possibility 10. canal(s) / channel / Channel 11. conduct / direct 12. continuous / continual 13. chauffeur / driver 14. wonderful / formidable 15. fun / funny 16. go / play 17. come along with / follow 18. damage / harm 19. discover / invent 20. work / job 21. kind / sympathetic 22. lie / lay 23. borrow / lend 24. nature / countryside 25. take / pass 26. practice / practise (in American English, *practice* can be both a noun and a verb) 27. priceless / valueless 28. principle / principal / principal / principle 29. rise / raise 30. receipt / recipe 31. remind / remember 32. scenery / view 33. sensitive / sensible 34. take / bring

1.   VERBS
1. chew 2. gulp 3. grate 4. steam 5. barbecue 6. marinade 7. nibble 8. swallow 9. gobble 10. baste 11. slice 12. fry 13. grill (in the USA = broil) 14. sip 15. chop 16. stir-fry 17. bake 18. dice 19. roast

2.   NOUNS
1. starter / main course / side dish / dessert 2. vegetarian / vegan 3. menu / bill / tip 4. diet / health foods / fast food 5. recipe / ingredients 6. takeaway

3.   IDIOMS, COLLOQUIALISMS AND OTHER EXPRESSIONS
The correct answers are:
1. a piece of cake 2. not my cup of tea 3. peanuts 4. the flavour of the month 5. trouble brewing 6. as red as a beetroot 7. the salt of the earth 8. bananas (we can also say *nuts*) 9. a butter fingers 10. chalk and cheese 11. spilled the beans 12. warm as toast 13. as cool as a cucumber 14. sour grapes 15. were packed together like sardines 16. a different kettle of fish

1.   VERBS
1. vandalised 2. mugged 3. burgled 4. robbed 5. stole 6. smuggled 7. falsified 8. trafficking 9. arrested 10. charged 11. tried 12. convicted 13. sentenced 14. break

2.   NOUNS

Criminal	Crime
a burglar	burglary
a robber	robbery
a shoplifter	shoplifting / shop theft
a vandal	vandalism
a rapist	rape
a hooligan	hooliganism
a murderer	murder
a hijacker	hijacking
a forger	forgery
a spy	spying / espionage
a pirate	piracy
a terrorist	terrorism

3.   NOUNS, VERBS AND ADJECTIVES
Look up the differences in your PCP English Dictionary for Students.

4.   IDIOMS, COLLOQUIALISMS AND OTHER EXPRESSIONS
1. thick as thieves 2. hardened 3. got away with 4. boys in blue / cops 5. boys in blue / cops 6. red handed 7. nicking 8. leg it 9. spill the beans 10. doing time / behind bars 11. nick 12. doing time / behind bars

1.   CHARACTER AND PERSONALITY
1. G 2. K 3. A 4. N 5. P 6. O 7. D 8. T 9. I 10. S 11. E 12. R 13. Q 14. H 15. J 16. C 17. M 18. L 19. B 20. F

2.   IDIOMS, COLLOQUIALISMS AND OTHER EXPRESSIONS
They are all negative except 9, 10, 11, 14, 16 and 22

1. VERBS
1 = C   2 = B   3 = A   4 = A   5 = B   6 = C   7 = B   8 = A   9 = B   10 = B

2. NOUNS
A.   1. pupil   2. student   3. degree   4. seminar   5. lecture   6. grant   7. tutorial   8. staff
9. graduate   10. subject   11. mark   12. state school   13. kindergarten

The word in the vertical strip is *undergraduate*.

B.
1.   A teacher works in a school. A professor works at a university.
2.   (In the UK) A primary school is for children aged 5 - 11. A secondary school is for children aged 11 - 16.
3.   A fee is the money you pay for your education. A grant is the money you receive from the government to help you pay for your education.
4.   A term is a period of study in a British school; there are three terms in a year. A semester is a period of study in a North American school; there are two semesters in a year.
5.   A graduate in Britain is someone who has successfully completed a course at university. A graduate in the USA is someone who has successfully completed a course at a high school (the US equivalent of a secondary school).
6.   A state school is run by the government and provides free education. A public school is independent and usually charges fees. The most famous example of a public school in Britain is Eton.

3. IDIOMS, COLLOQUIALISMS AND OTHER EXPRESSIONS
1. burn the candle at both ends   2. teacher's pet   3. pull your socks up   4. flunked (This word comes from the USA)

1. DEFINITIONS
1. P   2. B   3. N.   4. U.   5. O   6. H / J.   7. E   8. S   9. I   10. A   11. H / J   12. K.
13. T   14. D   15. M   16. G   17. R   18. C   19. L   20. F   21. Q

2. COMPLETE THE SENTENCES
1. get on like a house on fire   2. get a rise   3. Got it   4. got out of bed on the wrong side
5. getting me down   6. Get away   7. get to grips with   8. get-together   9. got a nerve
10. get lost / get knotted   11. get down to brass tacks   12. Get a grip on yourself
13. got the sack   14. get out of the habit of   15. Get lost / Get knotted   16. got on his nerves   17. getting nowhere   18. get off my back   19. get my act together   20. got my meaning   21. get going

1. VERBS
1. take exercise   2. keep fit   3. fall ill   4. look after   5. get well   6. cure   7. suffer
8. examine   9. treat   10. pick up   11. refer   12. operate   13. recuperate

2. NOUNS
A. Medical words
1. surgery   2. nurse   3. prescription   4. surgeon   5. casualty   6. patient   7. ward
8. psychiatrist   9. appointment   10. consultant   11. midwife   12. symptoms

p	p	r	e	s	c	r	i	p	t	i	o	n
s	c	a	s	u	a	l	t	y	c	k	a	p
s	p	s	m	r	s	c	a	n	p	y	p	w
c	w	w	p	g	e	g	b	d	f	j	p	s
p	a	t	i	e	n	t	w	z	y	p	o	y
a	r	b	c	r	u	d	e	f	g	t	i	m
r	d	q	p	y	r	o	n	m	l	b	n	p
s	t	c	o	n	s	u	l	t	a	n	t	t
q	s	u	r	g	e	o	n	m	m	s	m	o
i	o	i	y	r	m	i	d	w	i	f	e	m
y	j	h	g	f	d	s	a	z	x	c	n	s
p	s	y	c	h	i	a	t	r	i	s	t	x
w	o	p	i	u	y	t	r	f	d	s	a	c

B. Parts of the body.
1. forehead   2. eyebrow   3. cheek   4. nostrils   5. lips   6. Adam's apple   7. throat   8. shoulders   9. chest   10. stomach
11. waist   12. groin   13. hips   14. thighs   15. knee   16. shin   17. ankle   18. toes   19. sole

3. IDIOMS, COLLOQUIALISMS AND OTHER EXPRESSIONS

A. Feeling well / feeling ill.
1.☹ 2.☹ 3.☹ 4.☹ 5.☺ 6.☺ 7.☹ 8.☹ 9.☹

B. Parts of the body.
1. hand 2. elbow 3. leg 4. shoulder 5. thumb 6. eye 7. neck 8. foot 9. nose 10. ear

---

⇩ Human Actions. Pages 45-46

1. GENERAL ACTIONS
1. stretched 2. dragged 3. crouched 4. squatted 5. dived 6. leaned / leant 7. trembled 8. shivered 9. sweated
10. blushed 11. started 12. fainted 13. dozed 14. nodded 15. fidgeted

2. WAYS OF MOVING
A. stagger B. stroll C. leap D. march E. hop F. dash G. skip H. crawl I. creep / tiptoe J. creep / tiptoe K. dawdle

3. HAND AND ARM ACTIONS
1. punched 2. slapped 3. beckoned 4. stroked 5. patted 6. grabbed 7. grope 8. salute 9. waved 10. scratched
11. folded 12. wipe 13. shake 14. tapped 15. rubbed

4. IDIOMS, COLLOQUIALISMS AND OTHER EXPRESSIONS
1. False (she walked quickly) 2. True 3. False (the telephone isn't working properly)
4. True 5. True 6. True 7. False (we praise the firemen - we want to say that we think they are very brave) 8. False (don't criticize something which someone has given you for free) 9. True 10. False (his work is too easy and does not make him work as hard as he could) 11. False (everyone tried to get a ticket as quickly as possible) 12. True

---

⇩ Love And Relationships. Pages 47-48

1. A LOVE STORY part 1
1. attracted to 2. chatted her up 3. asked her out 4. wined and dined 5. got on 6. go out
7. courting 8. fallen in love 9. living in sin 10. cohabiting 11. proposed 12. got engaged
13. engagement 14. tie the knot 15. drift apart 16. split up

2. A LOVE STORY part 2
1. stag night 2. hen party 3. registry office 4. bride 5. groom 6. best man 7. wedding rings 8. Wedding March 9. aisle 10. bridesmaids 11. vows 12. wedding reception
13. toast 14. honeymoon

3. OTHER WORDS AND EXPRESSIONS
1 = G 2 = A 3 = J 4 = D 5 = E 6 = I 7 = L 8 = B 9 = K 10 = F 11 = C

⇩ Make or Do. Pages 49-50

1. WORDS USED WITH *MAKE* OR *DO*

1. made 2. does 3. did 4. making 5. made 6. done 7. making 8. do 9. doing 10. made 11. making 12. making
13. do 14. does 15. made 16. do 17. make 18. make 19. do 20. made 21. make 22. make 23. made 24. made
25. doing 26. made 27. doing 28. make

2. IDIOMS, COLLOQUIALISMS AND OTHER EXPRESSIONS USING *MAKE*
1. made off with 2. make do with a T-shirt 3. make the best of 4. make up my mind up
5. made a meal of repainting the kitchen 6. make-believe 7. make time 8. make a break with

3. IDIOMS, COLLOQUIALISMS AND OTHER EXPRESSIONS USING *DO*
1. trick 2. honours 3. dirty 4. wonders 5. yourself 6. without 7. turn 8. don'ts 9. turn 10. sights

r	t	d	y	u	i	t	e	w	q	f	h
l	w	i	t	h	o	u	t	k	s	g	f
w	e	i	r	t	u	r	o	p	i	g	h
l	k	t	j	d	o	n	t	s	g	c	v
m	y	y	t	y	r	s	u	c	h	v	b
w	o	n	d	e	r	s	r	m	t	n	b
m	u	n	b	v	c	x	n	e	s	r	t
p	r	o	i	u	y	t	r	e	w	q	a
b	s	n	b	v	c	t	r	i	c	k	d
e	e	d	e	w	d	f	g	h	j	k	l
x	l	l	k	h	o	n	o	u	r	s	n
c	f	j	h	g	f	d	s	a	b	v	c

1. ADJECTIVES AND NOUNS

1. cotton / polyester / leather / corduroy / denim   2. cardboard   3. corrugated iron
4. porcelain   5. turf   6. suede / leather / canvas   7. brick   8. wool   9. nylon / silk / satin
10. leather / cotton / denim / nylon   11. cork   12. polyester / satin / silk / cotton / denim / nylon   13. silk / satin   14. stained glass   15. fur / leather   16. plastic   17. cotton / satin / silk   18. linen / cotton   19. suede / canvas   20. stainless steel   21. timber   22. denim / cotton   23. rubber   24. wooden   25. iron   26. leather

2. GUESS THE OBJECT

1. a credit card   2. a saucepan   3. a tent   4. a cork (in a bottle of wine, for example)
5. an iron   6. a tie   7. jeans   8. a teapot   9. a scarf   10. a football

3. IDIOMS, COLLOQUIALISMS AND OTHER EXPRESSIONS

1. A   2. C   3. B   4. C   5. B   6. A   7. C   8. A

1.   VERBS

1. borrow   2. owe   3. earn   4. save   5. spend   6. lend   7. afford   8. pay back   9. bank
10. open   11. deposit   12. withdraw

2.   NOUNS

1.   Traditionally, a bank is a business organization which keeps money for customers and pays it out on demand or lends them money, and a building society is more usually associated with saving money or lending people money to buy houses.

2.   A current account is a bank account people use to cover everyday expenses, and a deposit account is used to save money (you usually need to give notice to withdraw money, but it pays a higher rate of interest.

3.   A withdrawal is when you take money from a bank account (verb = to withdraw). A deposit is when you put money into a bank account (verb = to deposit).

4.   A statement is a written record of the money you withdraw from and deposit into a bank account. A balance is a note which tells you how much money you have in your account.

5.   Cash is money (in the form of notes and coins). A cheque is specially printed sheet of paper supplied by a bank on which an order can be written.

6.   A credit card allows you to buy something from a shop and pay for it later. A debit card is a substitute for cash - money is taken directly from your bank account. A cheque guarantee card is a card that you use when you present a cheque and guarantees the shopkeeper that the cheque is valid.

7.   A bill tells you how much money you owe for, for example, a meal in a restaurant. A receipt is a written record of how much money you have spent in, for example, a shop.

8.   A standing order is an order to a bank to pay a fixed amount from an account to a named person or organization at a regular time each month, year etc. A direct debit is an order to a bank to pay money from your account to another account.

9.   A loan is money which is lent to you by a bank to buy something. An overdraft is when you spend more money that you have in your bank account without telling your bank beforehand.

1. building society   2. current account   3. withdrawal   4. balance   5. cheque   6. credit card   7. receipt   8. direct debit
9. overdraft

3.   IDIOMS, COLLOQUIALISMS AND OTHER EXPRESSIONS

3, 5, 11, 12, 15, 16 = you would probably feel <u>happy</u> about your financial situation.
1, 2, 4, 6, 7, 8, 9, 10, 13, 14, 17 = you would probably feel <u>unhappy</u> about your financial situation.

1. CLASSIFICATIONS

Mammals	Birds	Insects & invertebrates
human	swan	bee
squirrel	owl	ladybird
hedgehog	peacock	butterfly
leopard	parrot	wasp
deer	seagull	snail
dolphin	crow	beetle
whale	eagle	worm
bat	penguin	ant
	(A bat is not a bird; it does not lay eggs)	
Flowers	*Trees and other plants*	*Sea and river creatures*

rose marigold lily tulip orchid daffodil poppy daisy	cactus fir palm bamboo cedar oak mushroom seaweed	salmon squid shark crab lobster trout octopus oyster (You could also have included whales and dolphins in this category)

2. ANIMAL AND PLANT PARTS

pollen (P) wings (A) leaf (P) thorn (P) beak (A) bud (P) scales (A) gills (A) petal (P) whiskers (A) branch (P) paws (A) twig (P) trunk (P or A; see your dictionary for the definitions) claws (A) mane (A) stalk (P) hoof (A) root (P)

3. THE ENVIRONMENT

1. acid rain 2. recycle 3. fumes 4. pollution 5. greenhouse effect 6. C.F.C. 7. ozone layer 8. global warming 9. bottle bank 10. desertification 11. endangered 12. extinct 13. tidal energy / solar power

4. IDIOMS, COLLOQUIALISMS AND OTHER EXPRESSIONS

1. bird 2. bird 3. wolf 4. snail 5. butterflies 6. chickens 7. mule 8. elephant 9. fox 10. duck 11. donkey 12. bull

w	g	y	u	i	f	r	m	d	g	w	h
a	d	h	e	r	o	b	u	l	l	d	w
w	o	t	l	s	x	d	l	g	d	r	x
w	n	k	e	n	k	u	e	w	o	l	f
a	k	c	p	a	m	c	l	r	g	b	y
k	e	c	h	i	c	k	e	n	s	i	t
f	y	f	a	l	x	e	q	j	l	r	f
b	v	c	n	x	z	w	b	i	r	d	k
b	u	t	t	e	r	f	l	i	e	s	e

⇩ Noises. Pages 57-58

1. HUMAN NOISES

1. chant 2. whisper 3. puff / pant 4. pant 5. scream 6. stammer 7. snore 8. cough
9. sigh 10. boo 11. cheer 12. sniff 13. yawn 14. sneeze 15. groan 16. gasp

2. ANIMAL NOISES

croak = frog   squeak = mouse   howl = wolf   quack = duck   buzz = bee   grunt = pig
hiss = snake   neigh = horse   bray = donkey   bleat = sheep / goat   crow = cock
roar = lion   bark = dog   miaow / purr = cat

3. OTHER NOISES

1. pop 2. thud 3. blare 4. boom 5. ring 6. rattle 7. tinkle 8. clink 9. click / whirr
10. sizzle 11. rumble 12. murmur 13. bang 14. whirr

4. COMPLETE THE SENTENCES

1. gasped 2. chanted 3. snores 4. cheered 5. stammered 6. bleat 7. roared
8. barks 9. clicked 10. blaring 11. sizzled / popped 12. puffing / panting 13. sigh
14. purr

⇩ Opposites. Pages 59-60

1. VERBS

1. laughed 2. spend 3. succeeded 4. destroyed 5. depart / leave 6. emptied
7. hit 8. punish 9. forget 10. failed 11. received 12. win 13. lend 14. refused
15. defend 16. fallen 17. denied 18. forbidden / banned 19. loosened 20. retreated

2. ADJECTIVES

1. artificial 2. thick 3. lazy 4. sharp 5. amateur 6. tame 7. guilty 8. mean
9. light 10. hollow 11. soft 12. dim / thick 13. odd 14. tough 15. present 16. strong 17. light 18. permanent
19. high 20. high 21. stale 22. live 23. strong 24. shallow 25. smooth 26. compulsory 27. approximate 28. public 29. tough 30. smooth 31. soft / easy 32. soft 33. tight 34. sharp 35. live 36. dim / thick 37. easy 38. light 39. stale 40. minor 41. cool 42. cool

1.   SHAPE

A.

1.E   2.D   3.J   4.F   5.A   6.G   7.H   8.K   9.I   10.B   11.C

B. 1. spherical   2. cubed   3. conical   4. rectangular   5. triangular   6. circular   7. square   8. cylindrical

2.   SIZE

Big	Small
enormous mammoth huge gigantic monumental colossal massive giant gargantuan	minute minuscule tiny titchy teeny (These last two are colloquial and often used by small children)

3.   FEATURES

1. D   2. F   3. H   4. G   5. I   6. B   7. E   8. A   9. C

1.   VERBS

1 = B   2 = A   3 = C   4 = C   5 = A   6 = B   7 = C

2.   NOUNS

A.   1 = C   2 = F   3 = D   4 = H   5 = G   6 = B   7 = E   8 = A

B.   1. refound = refund   2. bargein = bargain   3. sails = sales   4. male = mail   5. reciept = receipt   6. lapel = label
7. cashear = cashier

C.   A *packet* of biscuits   A *jar* of jam   A *bar* of chocolate   A *tube* of toothpaste   A *box* of matches   A *tin* of soup.

The word in the vertical strip is *carton* (eg a carton of fruit juice)

3.   IDIOMS, COLLOQUIALISMS AND OTHER EXPRESSIONS

1. A large amount   2. A large amount   3. A large amount   4. A small amount   5. A large amount   6. A small amount.

1. False   2. False   3. True   4. False   5. False   6. False

1. VERBS.

1. C   2. A   3. B   4. C   5. A   6. C   7. C   8. A   9. B   10. A

2. NOUNS

A. Venues and equipment.

swimming - pool - trunks
tennis - court - racket
football - pitch - strip
ice-hockey - rink - stick
horse-racing - racecourse - saddle
shooting - range - target
motor-racing - racetrack - helmet
boxing - ring - gloves

B. Jumbled words.

stadium   referee   umpire   linesman   spectator   player   athlete   scoreboard   supporter   arena

3. IDIOMS, COLLOQUIALISMS AND OTHER EXPRESSIONS.

1. darts   2. motor-racing   3. horse-racing (we can also use this expression for any game or sport where two or more players or teams have the same score or are in equal position)   4. athletics (before running a race)   5. boxing   6. football (we can also use this word for any other game in which one player deliberately tries to stop another player from winning a game)
7. golf

The word in the shaded vertical strip is *Arsenal*, a football team from North London.

1.   VERBS
A.   (Sentences in the correct order):
1.   I picked up some brochures from the travel agency.
2.   I browsed through the brochures.
3.   I chose the holiday I wanted.
4.   I then booked my holiday.
5.   A few weeks later I went to the airport and checked in for my flight.
6.   I did some shopping in the duty free and then boarded my flight.
7.   I found my seat and fastened my safety belt.
8.   The flight took off at 10 o'clock
9.   Three hours later we landed.
10.   All the passengers disembarked.
11.   I left the airport and two hours later arrived at my hotel, where I checked in.
12.   I spent the next two weeks sunbathing on the beach and sightseeing in the local area.
13.   It was with a great deal of reluctance that I eventually checked out of the hotel and returned home.

B.
These people like travelling: Bob, Jo, Mark, Eric.
These people dislike travelling: Bazil, Jane, Penny, Elsa, Vicky.

2.   NOUNS
A.   Suggested answers:
1.   a package holiday = a hotel, a resort, a villa / chalet.
2.   a camping holiday = a tent, a caravan
3.   a cruise = a ship's cabin
4.   a skiing holiday = a hotel, a resort, a youth hostel, a guest house, a chalet
5.   a safari = a tent, a hotel, a resort
6.   a walking holiday = a tent, a hotel, a youth hostel, a guest house.
7.   a sailing holiday = a boat's cabin
8.   a caravanning holiday = a caravan
9.   a sightseeing holiday = a hotel, a youth hostel, a guest house

B.
1. excursion   2. voyage   3. tour   4. journey   5. trip   6. travel agency / tour operator
7. aisle   8. boarding card (boarding pass)   9. passport / insurance / traveller's cheques / foreign currency / suitcase / shoulder bag

3.   IDIOMS, COLLOQUIALISMS AND OTHER EXPRESSIONS
1. D   2. H   3. B   4. F   5. G   6. I   7. J   8. C   9. A   10. E

⇩ **24 Hours. Pages 69-70**

1.   VERBS
1. C   2. B   3. A   4. A   5. C   6. A   7. B   8. B

2.   NOUNS

Things we use / wear at home	Things we use / wear at work
shaver pyjamas nightie iron tumble drier ironing board kettle refrigerator vacuum cleaner hair dryer dishwasher hairbrush microwave oven slippers dressing gown apron	ring binder computer filing cabinet file business card briefcase fax e-mail suit internet (Of course, you might use some of the things on the left at work too)

B.   1. e-mail / fax   2. dishwasher   3. pyjamas / slippers   4. hair dryer   5. briefcase   6. fax
7. kettle   8. microwave

3.   IDIOMS, COLLOQUIALISMS AND OTHER EXPRESSIONS
A.   1. J   2. D   3. I   4. L   5. B   6. K   7. C   8. F   9. H   10. A   11. E   12. G

B.   1. take my time   2. time's up   3. At times   4. in time (we can also say in the nick of time)   5. on time   6. behind
     the times   7. time after time   8. waste time   9. pressed for time   10. For the time being

⇩ **Weather And Natural Phenomena. Pages 71-72**

1.   BAD WEATHER
1. rain   2. wind   3. hail   4. thunder   5. lightning   6. fog   7. mist   8. smog   9. frost
10. snow / sleet   11. snow / sleet   12. blizzard

2.	EXTREME WEATHER AND OTHER NATURAL PHENOMENA
1. B (in the Caribbean or Eastern Pacific Ocean. In the Far East, it is called a *typhoon*. In the Indian Ocean it is called a *cyclone*) 2. C   3. C   4. C   5. A   6. B   7. B (the word is Japanese in origin. We also say *tidal wave*)

3.	WEATHER WORD FORMS

NOUN	VERB	ADJECTIVE
rain	rain / pour	rainy
sun	shine	sunny
storm	storm	stormy
snow	snow	snowy
wind	blow / howl	windy

4.	IDIOMS, COLLOQUIALISMS AND OTHER EXPRESSIONS
1. cats and dogs   2. bucketing down   3. boiling (we can also say *roasting* or *sweltering*)
4. heavy weather of it   5. under the weather   6. downpour   7. weather   8. Every cloud has a silver lining (an English proverb)   9. on cloud nine   10. under a cloud   11. steals my thunder   12. a storm in a teacup

⇩ Work. Pages 73-74

1.	VERBS
1. hand in his notice   2. apply for   3. dismissed   4. resign   5. retire   6. filled in   7. promoted   8. attend an interview
9. commute   10. laid off

2.	NOUNS
1. vacancy   2. salesperson   3. employee   4. candidates   5. qualifications / references   6. qualifications / references
7. short-list   8. candidates   9. salary   10. increment   11. commission   12. perks   13. pension   14. promotion
15. manager   16. prospects

3.	IDIOMS, COLLOQUIALISMS AND OTHER EXPRESSIONS
1. C   2. M   3. I   4. J   5. F   6. H   7. P   8. B   9. D   10. G   11. L   12. A   13. K   14. E   15. O   16. N

⇩ Come / Cut. Page 75

Phrasal verbs with *come*
1. D   2. A   3. B   4. K   5. J   6. C   7. G   8. H   9. I   10. F   11. E

Phrasal verbs with *cut*
1. cut back   2. cut down on   3. cut off   4. cut in   5. cut in   6. cut out   7. cut off

⇩ Do / Get. Pages 75-76

Phrasal verbs with *do*
1. do away with   2. do in (or do away with)   3. do up   4. do it up   5. could do with
6. do in   7. do without

Phrasal verbs with *get*
1. I   2. M   3. N   4. A   5. D   6. E   7. O   8. P   9. F   10. B   11. H   12. J   13. K   14. L   15. G   16. C

⇩ Give / Go. Pages 76-77

Phrasal verbs with *give*
1. away   2. away   3. out   4. out   5. up   6. up   7. in   8. off

Phrasal verbs with *go*
1. correct   2. off   3. off   4. correct   5. on   6. out   7. correct   8. down   9. up
10. correct   11. correct   12. about   13. correct   14. on   15. correct   16. correct

⇩ Look / Make. Pages 77-78

Phrasal verbs with *look*
1. looking forward to   2. looking up   3. look out over   4. looks down on   5. Look out!
6. looks up to   7. Look me up   8. looked over   9. look into   10. look after   11. looking out for

Phrasal verbs with *make*
1. G   2. E   3. F   4. B   5. D   6. C   7. A

Phrasal verbs with *pick*
1. A   2. B   3. C   4. C   5. A   6. B

Phrasal verbs with *put*
1. put by (we can also say *put aside*)   2. put off   3. put...off   4. put down   5. put through
6. put up with   7. put...down   8. put...down   9. put...up

Phrasal verbs with *run*
1. G   2. E   3. I   4. K   5. J   6. A   7. C   8. D   9. L   10. F   11. H   12. B

Phrasal verbs with *set*
1. False - you have just started it   2. True   3. false - you have just started a company
4. False - you have just moved into a new home   5. True   6. false - your journey has been delayed   7. False - you have just lost some money on, eg, a bad business deal   8. True   9. False - you save it   10. False - you start doing it.

Phrasal verbs with *take*
1. B   2. C   3. A   4. B   5. C   6. C   7. B

Phrasal verbs with *turn*
turn down: a job   the heat on a cooker   a television   applicants for a job   (a light, if it is used with a dimmer switch)
turn into: a road
turn out: cars in a factory   people from a house because they haven't paid the rent   guests at a party
turn away: people from a restaurant because it's full
turn off: a road   a radio   a light   a television
turn over: the page of a book   money
turn up: a lost child
turn on: a television   a light   a radio

1. The lift has **broken down** again.
2. I'm trying to **work out** if we've sold more this year than last year.
3. After walking across the USA, his boots were **worn out**.
4. The effects of the drug **wore off** after a few hours.
5. She **wore** herself **out** looking after the old lady.
6. She **pulled through**, thanks to the help of the specialists
7. Did you **sort out** the problem of the hotel bill?
8. They had an argument and **split up**.
9. We invited all our friends to the picnic, but it rained and only five of them **showed up**.
10. A car **pulled up** and the driver asked me if I wanted a lift.
11. Our Australian partners **pulled out** at the last moment.
12. The terrorists **let off** guns in the street.
13. The people I asked to speak at the meeting **let** me **down**.
14. It will be marvellous if we **pull it off**.
15. The cars **carried on** even though the road was covered with snow.
16. The planes were **held up** by fog.
17. **Hold on (Hang on).**, I'll get my umbrella.
18. Don't watch her dancing like that - she's just **showing off**.
19. Our planned holiday in Spain **fell through** because we had too much work at the office.
20. After the movie, we all **ended up** at my girlfriend's flat.
21. Doctors **carried out** some tests on the patients.
22. They **carried on** working, even though the office was on fire.
23. He **fell behind** with his mortgage repayments.
24. She **called on** her mother to see how she was.
25. The oil tanker was **breaking up** on the rocks.
26. They **fell out** over the bill for the drinks.
27. He had to **face up to** the unpleasant fact that he was never going to be rich.
28. He decided to **call off** the visit to the museum.
29. Can I **count on** you to help wash the dishes?
30. Burglars **broke into** the office during the night.

1. came across   2. do with   3. set in   4. took over   5. picked...up   6. put by / away   7. takes after   8. turned...down
9. went off   10. cut off   11. run / go through   12. put back   13. pick up   14. give up   15. put...through   16. ran into
17. made up   18. went on   19. look forward   20. cut down   21. do without   22. broke into   23. made up   24. do up
25. looked after   26. gone up   27. giving away   28. broken down   29. came through   30. getting on   31. turn...away

PRACTICE 1

	practise		here		nothing
	After		chewing		speak
	college		books		group
	criticize		come		nice
	around		remember		should
	hire		Students		night
	our		them		teacher
	door		enjoyable		Loch
	noise		For		thank
	residential		background		living
	aware		help		walk
	make		you		comes
	cultural		complain		leisure
	throw		block		
	keep		problems		
	respect		not		

PRACTICE 2

full = wood   catch = kettle   anchor = abroad   cello = cheers   zoo = choose   hare = bear   bean = peek   course = hall
sun = certain   money = hum   fun = phoney   boys = hoist   flow = boat   tie = buy   mouse = now   crate / clay = plate / great
through = lose   large = can't   beer = ear

1. beard   2. bead   3. threat   4. fear   5. beak   6. horse   7. height   8. home   9. bomb   10. few   11. town   12. bear
13. mould   14. peace   15. said   16. foul   17. wool   18. gone   19. thwart   20. watch   21. choose   22. wander
23. work   24. foot   25. vase

○◆ (eg, pro**duce** (verb))	◆○ (eg, **pro**duce (noun))
employ	present (noun)
present (verb)	rebel (noun)
rebel (verb)	answer (noun and verb)
depart	suspect (noun)
discuss	massage (noun)
suspect (verb)	conduct (noun)
compute	decrease (noun)
guitar	fortune
obscene	contact (noun and verb)
massage (verb)	attempt (noun and verb)
conduct (verb)	
decrease (verb)	
decide	
◆○○ (eg, **photo**graph)	○◆○ (eg, es**tab**lish)
advertise	employee
operate	departure
indicate	discussion
sympathy	computer
sympathise	guitarist
luxury	electric
origin	decision
decorate	
fortunate	

○○◆ (eg, discon**tent**)	◆○○○ (eg, **I**rishwoman)
disagree	operator
	indicator
	decorator
	fortunately
○◆○○ (eg, pho**tog**raphy)	○○◆○ (eg, re-es**tab**lish)
advertisement	disagreement
unfortunate	economics
economise	operation
luxurious	indication
original	sympathetic
obscenity	
○○◆○○ (eg, unpro**nounc**able)	○◆○○○ (eg, un**ques**tionable)
electricity	unfortunately

⇩ Same Spelling / Same Pronunciation / Different Meaning. Pages 88-89

PUNS

1. bright   2. change   3. atmosphere   4. charge   5. bar   6. horns   7. beat   8. count   9. patient   10. Call

WORDSEARCH

1. can   2. wave   3. grave   4. mean   5. cool   6. bank   7. coach   8. ring   9. light   10. match

⇩ Same Pronunciation / Different Spelling / Different Meaning. Pages 90-91

1.
1. deer   2. brake   3. fate   4. grate   5. mail   6. naval   7. pain   8. paced   9. sale   10. stakes   11. stationery   12. suede
13. tale   14. wail   15. waist

2. King of the Jungle
The correct words are in bold.

KING OF THE JUNGLE

Larry the lion was very fierce and all the other animals in the jungle were afraid of him. He had always **been** very proud of this fact.
One day, while he was out walking, who should he **meet** but Morris the monkey. Larry stopped him before he could **flee**.
"Who's the King of the jungle, little monkey?" asked Larry.
"Uh, **you** are." replied Morris the monkey, and quickly ran away, putting several hundred **metres** between himself and Larry.
Larry continued walking until he came across Bert the **bear**.
"Hey you! Who's the King of the jungle?" demanded Larry.
"You are, so I **hear**," replied Bert, cautiously backing into the bushes.
Feeling very pleased with himself, Larry continued walking until he bumped into Dave the **deer**. Larry **caught** him by the antlers before he could escape
"Who's the King of the jungle?" asked Larry?
"You're such a well-**bred** animal, it must be you," **whined** Dave. This pleased Larry and he **allowed** Dave to walk away. He carried on walking until he **saw** Gary the gorilla sitting in his tree.
"Hey you, ugly, who's the King of the jungle?" asked Larry.
Gary ignored him, so Larry let out a deafening **roar**.
"I said, who's the King of the jungle, you stupid gorilla?"
Gary climbed down from his tree, walked up to Larry, hit him over the head with a piece of **wood**, picked him up, **threw** him on the ground and jumped up and down on him. He then climbed back into his tree.
Larry looked up at him and said "All right. There's no need to get angry just because you don't **know** the answer"